# Total
# Exposure

# Total Exposure

## Controlling Your Company's Image in the Glare of the Business Media Explosion

GUSTAV CARLSON

## AMACOM

American Management Association

New York • Atlanta • Boston • Chicago • Kansas City • San Francisco • Washington, D.C.

Brussels • Mexico City • Tokyo • Toronto

This publication is designed to provide accurate and authoritative information in regard to the subject matter covered. It is sold with the understanding that the publisher is not engaged in rendering legal, accounting, or other professional service. If legal advice or other expert assistance is required, the services of a competent professional person should be sought.

Library of Congress Cataloging-in-Publication Data

Carlson, Gustav.
    Total exposure: controlling your company's image in the glare of the business media explosion/ Gustav Carlson. Carlson.
        p.  cm.
    Includes index.
    ISBN 0-8144-0484-7
    1. Corporate image—United States. 2. Public relations—United States. 3. Industrial publicity—United States. I. Title.
    HD59.2.C366  1999
    659.2—dc21
                                        99-40039
                                        CIP

Printing number

10  9  8  7  6  5  4  3  2  1

*To my Father, a newspaperman, who
taught me that a reporter's
relationship with readers is a privilege,
not a right.*

# CONTENTS

Preface   ix

Acknowledgments   xi

1   **The Rise of the Consumer-Investor:**
*A New View of Corporate America*   **1**

2   **Barbie in the Boardroom:**
*Business News as Entertainment*   **17**

3   **The Dumbing Down of News:**
*A Talent Deficit Grows*   **35**

4   **Filling the Space:**
*The Credibility Vacuum*   **53**

5   **Gen-X Journalism:**
*The Mouse That Roared*   **67**

6   **The "Me" Media:**
*Online's Darker Side*   **87**

7   **The Reluctant Media Darling:**
*Lessons From Wall Street*   **105**

8   **Who's Out There?**
*The Media's Audiences Are Your Customers*   **125**

9   **The Kid in the Candy Store:**
*Overcoming the Temptations of Plenty*   **145**

**10  Above the Clatter:**
*What to Say and Who Should Say It*                                      **163**

**11  Know the Enemy:**
*The Chink in the PR Armor*                                              **181**

**12  Hitting the Iceberg:**
*Adding Media to Your Crisis Plan*                                       **199**

**Conclusion**                                                          **219**

**Index**                                                               **221**

# PREFACE

The idea for this book was born at lunch in a midtown Manhattan restaurant in the mid-1990s. My guest that day was a friend who was doing public relations work for a small pharmaceutical company that made generic drugs. While we ate and chatted, we also kept our eyes on the television in the corner of the room, where the financial television network CNBC was broadcasting its noon-hour news. Among the guests on the program was the president of a high-technology company whose leading product had apparently not lived up to expectations. A competitor had brought to market a superior product, this fellow's stock had tanked, and he was on the hot seat on national TV, doing his best at damage control. My friend was riveted by the real-life drama. "Thank God my client's so small that no one knows who he is or what he does," she said, finally. "I wouldn't want him to be where that guy is right now."

Not long after, my friend was on the phone to me. Her client's worst nightmare had come true. A large competitor had sued the F.D.A. for approving her client's company's generic version of a brand name drug and was bad-mouthing the knock-off in the process. The competitor had also won a stay from the court that stopped shipment of her client's only product. The Wall Street Journal had picked up the story. Overnight, her client's company had gone from comfortable obscurity to national infamy. The incident not only threatened the company's reputation, but its existence as well. The company was, in effect, totally exposed.

The story has a happy ending, but only because my friend's counsel to her client was expert. She helped him tell *The Wall Street Journal* and other news media his company's side of the story, carefully and completely. The client addressed and successfully refuted the competitor's claims, producing supporting evidence about the virtues of the drug that had also impressed the F.D.A. in the approval process. In the end, the case was thrown out and the company resumed shipping its product. But the lesson was clear. In the new media environment, there is nowhere for companies to hide, no matter how small they are.

That said, it is important to understand that this book is not about media bashing. Nor is it about business bashing. Either exercise would be too easy—and it would have little value to anyone who wants to understand more about the increasingly dynamic relationship between companies and the news media that covers them. A company that blames the news media for creating or contributing to its problems is playing the biggest cop-out game in Corporate America. A reporter who blames a company for trying to promote or protect itself through public relations—and thereby somehow obscuring "truth"—is failing to understand that a company's main reasons for being are to survive and succeed, not to cater to the news media's agenda.

In between what a company wants and what a reporter wants lies the issue that is the focus of this book. It is, quite simply, a knowledge gap. Many companies, particularly young ones, don't know how to tell their stories to the media properly. Many reporters, particularly those new to the business beat, don't know enough about the complexities of business to make sense of information and give it meaning for their audiences. Complicating the process is technology, which gives both sides the false impression that the ability to move more and more information around the world 24 hours a day is useful. Without context, this information overload is far from useful—it is confusing. Add to this a growing hunger for insight, not simply information, from a new generation of Americans who are taking more responsibility for their financial futures, and the knowledge gap becomes even wider.

Companies that understand the gap and take steps to close it will see benefits. Most established companies that have been around the media for some time get the point. But many young, small companies, particularly those that are newly public, may not yet have caught on to the issue. They haven't learned how to promote or protect themselves. It is to these companies, especially, and the executives who run them, that this book is directed.

# ACKNOWLEDGMENTS

So many people contributed so much to this book that any attempt on my part to convey in a few words the importance of their efforts and my gratitude to them would fall short. Friends, family, critics, business associates, clients and journalists all had hands in the project, contributing ideas, anecdotes, guidance and editing copy. Among the most influential: Edward Hersh, a senior producer for A&E, a former producer for ABC News, a colleague at Hill and Knowlton, and a good friend, whose fascination with the knowledge gap between business and the news media mirrors my own; Donald Marron, chairman and chief executive officer of PaineWebber, who put into perspective for me the remarkable changes in business that generated my thesis; Donna Peterman, my former boss at both PaineWebber and Hill and Knowlton, who endured my journalist's skepticism about "spin" and taught me that public relations done well is a powerful and legitimate business tool; Jim Taylor, former head of Hill and Knowlton's New York office, who inspired me with his conviction that creative thinking and business need each other; and journalists like Rex Seline, a former editor for *The New York Times* and my boss at *The Miami Herald*, who schooled me on the big leagues of journalism. Then there are the characters I met along the way—the subjects of newspaper stories I covered, the clients I served, the colleagues with whom I worked—who supplied me with so much rich material from which to draw and, in some cases, allowed me to use their work as supporting evidence for my thesis. I would also like to thank Christina McLaughlin for her painstaking work in overseeing the production of this book. And, of course, there is my editor, Ellen Kadin, whose professional support and friendship helped bring it all together. There are many more people in the recent and distant past who inspired, encouraged and challenged me to look for bigger ideas. To all of them, my sincere thanks.

# Total Exposure

# CHAPTER 1

# The Rise of the Consumer-Investor:

## A New View of Corporate America

I f you run a public company—small, midsize, or large—consider this a wake-up call. Things have changed in the business news media. And they have changed almost overnight. Business news isn't the sleepy, stodgy world of newspaper stock tables it was ten, even five years ago. It is a highly charged, aggressive universe that has grown to the point where it is among the most influential audiences for companies, mainly because other influential audiences such as customers, shareholders, financial analysts, and employees use it as their main source of information and opinion. If yours is a large company, you probably are aware of this new dynamic and are doing something to manage it, either by having your own employees handle it or with a public relations firm you've hired. If yours is a small or midsize company, you may not be as tuned in—but you need to be. You must pay attention to what is happening in the business news environment because the business news is paying attention to you.

Don't believe it? Look around. Turn on the television. There are CNBC, CNN/fn, and Bloomberg television delivering twenty-four-hour, seven-days-a-week business and financial news about public companies small, medium, and large. The major broadcast networks and cable competitors such as CNN and Fox deliver more business news as part of their programming than ever before. At the newsstand, all kinds of business publications are on display— the usual old standards as well as a bunch of new entries, many of which concentrate on personal finance and investment. Even lifestyle publications contain heavy doses of business news.

Now, go online. The proliferation of news services and investment sites on the Internet is staggering. And if you have a second computer terminal on your desk, it's probably a Bloomberg offering all business, all the time.

Think back ten years—even five—and you'll begin to get a sense of how much things have changed. Ten years ago, business news was nowhere. Now, it's everywhere. Average Americans are thinking about business, talking about business. And the news media are delivering more information about business to feed this growing demand. Whether you like it or not, you are part of this phenomenon. Understanding the reasons this is happening and figuring out how to manage the change are important to your business.

Why listen to me? I've had a unique view of the business news media revolution—as a journalist with newspapers like *The New York Times* and *The Miami Herald*, as a media specialist with the global public relations agency Hill & Knowlton, as a corporate spokesman for the major Wall Street firm PaineWebber Incorporated, and as an independent consultant to Fortune 500 companies and smaller public companies alike. As a journalist, I understand the news gathering process, editors' agendas, and reporters' motives. As a media strategist, I know the challenges compaines face getting their stories into the media and proteting themselves in a crisis. And as a corporate spokesman, I know what it's like to be on the front line of news, positive and negative. Despite this broad experience, I am always aware that managing the media is not an exact science. It is a moving target. Your company needs to understand this, especially in the new business news environment, because it is moving mighty fast.

Here's why it's happening. Today Americans are forced to assume responsibility for their future financial well-being. This new breed of individuals—call them consumer-investors—no longer sees companies simply as makers of products or providers of services. Consumer-investors also see companies as potential investments that will help to finance everything from their children's college education to retirement security. They need information to make sound financial decisions. They want details, analysis, and insight about what makes a company tick, not just about what it makes. In effect, they want the context that turns information into knowledge. And they want it twenty-four hours a day, every day of the year, wherever they may be. Conventional company methods of building brand awareness and loyalty, such as advertising and marketing, do not provide that kind of information.

Enter the business news media. With this new national obsession with investing, business news has become one of the hottest media sectors in the country, fostering unprecedented growth in business journalism during the last decade. Newspapers, news wires, television, specialty magazines, newsletters, news radio, and online services have quickly become the main sources of information for the consumer-investor, who is hungry for an edge and sophisticated enough to employ every technological means possible to get it. The old guard, such as *The Wall Street Journal, The New York Times,* and *Business Week,* cannot satisfy this hunger alone. The consumer-investor feasts on CNBC, CNN, Fox News, *Barron's, Smart Money, Kiplinger's,* TheStreet.com, and an array of publications and Web sites you may never even have hear of.

Successful companies are learning to adapt their self-promotion to this change because the media are paying attention to them whether they like it or not. These companies realize their role is to provide the context that will help the consumer-investor make knowledgeable investment decisions. Smart companies understand that because the learning curve of the consumer-investor is steep, and the clatter caused by so many voices conveying so much information can be confusing, they must educate as well as inform. And they must use the media to do it because the media have become the crossroads at which companies and consumer-investors meet. The bottom line: Effective use of the media can not only increase sales but also boost stock prices. Ignorance or misuse of the media will have the opposite effect on both fronts.

As Americans assume responsibility for their financial health and future, consumers are turning to investing to win financial security for themselves. This trend has reshaped the financial markets in the United States and, through this country's immense influence, in markets around the world. It prompted Donald B. Marron, chairman and chief executive officer of PaineWebber Group Inc., a large New York-based investment securities firm, to call the 1990s the decade of the individual investor. The unprecedented bull market run of the late 1990s, fueled mainly by the inflow of money from individuals, proved his thesis. With the move of companies away from defined benefit plans to defined contribution plans and the growing concerns about the long-term reliability of Social Security, investing has become an essential part of financial and retirement planning rather than simply an exercise for wealthy speculators and institutions. Studies commissioned by PaineWebber and conducted by The Gallup Organization reveal that one-third of all Americans now consider themselves investors, with at least $10,000 invested in assets such as 401(k) plans, mutual funds, and Individual Retirement Accounts (IRAs). In effect, Marron said, the shift has created a nation of pension fund managers, adding that few are qualified for the job.

Add to this the demographic trends, and the foundation of the business media explosion becomes clearer. As the members of the baby boom generation prepare for retirement, they are transforming themselves from spenders into savers. More sophisticated than their parents about investing and increasingly comfortable with the technology that allows them to cruise around the world on the Internet looking for investment opportunities, the baby boomers are pouring billions of dollars into the financial markets. Their goal: to ensure financial security at retirement and preempt the need to rely on a Social Security system they believe is doomed to fail unless some sort of reform is achieved.

The business media is acutely aware of their huge role in the rise of the consumer investor. A May 1999 article in *The New York*

*Times*—a traditional source of investment information—noted the spectacular impact that new media sources like the Internet are having. In it, writer Robert D. Hershey examined the growth of Internet stock trading as a way Americans are goofing off at work. Hershey cited a Florida dentist who tracks stocks between patient treatments, a Washington freight company manager who logs on to a financial Web site for four to six hours of his work day, and a California architectural designer whose productivity has fallen 25 percent because of his involvement with the stock market. "The long bull market and cascading advances in technology have combined to drive capitalism's main numbers game into the heart of the American workplace, with millions of wage earners, managers and entrepreneurs obsessing about Wall Street," Hershey wrote. "Their obsession, in fact, far eclipses the speculative 1920s, when elevator operators and bootblacks were the chief source of what passed for information."

This insatiable hunger for information, not only about financial markets but also about the companies and institutions that fuel them, is expected to continue in the United States for another decade or more as baby boomers approach and pass into retirement. Other parts of the world are not far behind. Germany, France, and the United Kingdom are already seeing similar signs of a shift in financial responsibility to the individual. Changes in laws have resulted in the growth of mutual funds in Japan, and other parts of Asia will likely follow that country's example. China has huge potential to become a massive nation of individual investors as well despite political and social hurdles.

In their demand for financial information, Americans have become critical consumers of business news. Studies show that they are more skeptical and less likely to take advertisers' messages at face value. Advertising has become an awareness builder, a tickler for consumers who increasingly seek third-party endorsement before making purchasing decisions. James Taylor, a marketing and branding guru and author of *The 500-Year Delta: What Happens After What Comes Next,* calls the phenomenon the "Siskel and Ebertizing of America," referring to the pair of popular movie critics to whom millions of followers turned for recommendations on blockbusters and flops. If a company and its products don't get the critics' trade-mark "two thumbs up" from an independent expert, the company has a problem.

The growth of the consumer-investor and the business news media have had a powerful impact on the financial services indus-try, transforming it almost overnight from a small, exclusive club into a mass consumer business. Suddenly, more millions of people than ever want to know what products these firms are offering and how they stack up as investments as well as what they think about other companies as places to park their money. Wall Street firms are getting exposure three times over—first, as companies from which the consumer-investor may want to buy products and services; sec-ond, as investments in themselves; and third, as advisors on the investment potential of other companies. Chief executives of banks and brokerage firms who once were rarely seen in public are now all over the media talking about their companies, the market, the economy, and world events. Research analysts have become stars, offering advice, participating in stock-picking contests, and spend-ing as much time in front of television cameras as they do research-ing the companies they cover. Some financial firms have welcomed the media attention; others appear to be reluctant media darlings, dragged into the spotlight and suffering from more than a little stage fright. The lessons they have learned are valuable for every industry.

The upshot: The new business media environment of today is a far more dynamic place than the Dark Ages of not so long ago when only a handful of media outlets paid attention to business. The best known media then were *The Wall Street Journal, The New York Times, Forbes, Fortune, Business Week, Barron's* and, to a lesser extent, the now-defunct *Financial World*. In those days, there were no broadly watched television programs, few specialized personal finance magazines, and no online networks. Local newspapers paid lip service to business news, and their financial pages consisted mainly of stock tables. The business desks of these newspapers were the dumping grounds for tired editors and reporters who could not get into too much trouble if they made mistakes because few readers cared about business news. And because financial news was so far out of the mainstream, a negative story was pretty much a yawn for the average American.

But as alluring as the new media environment may be for companies anxious to make news, it is a two-edged sword, especially for growing companies that need to educate as well as inform. On the plus side, the democratization of information provides many more direct channels to the consumer-investor. The opportunities for companies to get out their messages have never been better or more plentiful. There are wider and more diverse audiences whose flagging confidence in advertising has made editorial coverage a prime third-party endorsement that influences purchasing and investing decisions. Technology allows fast, targeted, and customized dissemination of news and instant feedback from audiences. Taking the pulse of the market has never been easier. Companies not only can send out data, they can instantly receive it back from the field. Providing context that quickly turns information into knowledge is possible, though not yet effective, on a wide basis.

For large companies, there are now more ways to use spokespeople without overexposing chief executives and other senior managers. Small companies that understand and use the media can build the kind of recognition usually reserved for large, established companies that get attention because they can move markets. And they can do it on a relatively cost-effective basis, because good public relations is a fraction of the cost of advertising. In effect, this change has opened new and inexpensive ways to see and be seen. Companies that will never be mentioned in *The Wall Street Journal* because they are too small now have myriad other opportunities to reach broad audiences.

Of course, there is danger in a company overexposing itself. It may sound like a cliché of the hired guns who are hired to handle the media, but the quality of coverage is far more important than the quantity of coverage. It doesn't simply matter what you say, but where you say it. To get maximum impact, a company needs to target the media to which its key audiences turn most often for information and insight. In that way, effective media relations are not that different from other sales methods.

The top executive who ignores the media in a crisis, such as when a product fails or a catastrophe affects production, does so at his own peril. You have more prying eyes on your and your company. Placing a premium on speedy delivery, reporters often move information without waiting for context. At some online news services, they have no choice. Computer systems are programmed to give reporters and editors a set amount of time to work on stories, after which the articles are posted publicly, whether or not the facts have been checked. With no perspective, or an incorrect perspective, investors can misinterpret events. Mountains can quickly become molehills. Miscues are uncovered and spread with blinding speed around the world, twenty-four hours a day. Information, accurate and inaccurate, can snowball before a company even knows it is in the public eye. Crises are more likely to occur and less likely to be easily contained.

If you run a small company, you are even more vulnerable in this environment because, unlike big companies, you probably don't have the financial resources or consumer brand loyalty to survive a serious hit. That's not to say that a well-known brand is insurance against bad publicity. Ask the Intel Corporation. The computer chip maker was right in the middle of a $150-million brand-building advertising campaign when rumblings began in online chat rooms about flaws in its Pentium chip. Intel, for reasons that remain a mystery, misjudged the growing influence of Internet chat rooms and did not react. The news quickly spread through other media, and suddenly the company had a full-fledged crisis on its hands. A series of public relations blunders, all intended to downplay the problem, escalated into one of the biggest catastrophes involving a company's reputation in recent corporate history. It ended with Intel's chief executive officer, Andrew Grove, admitting that the company had been arrogant in its refusal to acknowledge the mistake immediately and replace the defective parts. In the end, Intel stock dropped two percent and the company launched a new advertising campaign that simply said, "We apologize."

In the new media environment, sloppy management of a company's profile is not the only pitfall. There are problems inherent in this new environment. Like any industry that expands quickly, the business news media have had their growing pains. While the demand for insight and analysis grows, the industry suffers from a deficit of talent. The dangers are obvious when inexperienced reporters try to provide investment advice about your company to the hungry consumer-investor audience. A bull market gives them perfect cover. At a time when a blindfolded novice can beat the S&P 500 by throwing darts at the stock table pages of *The Wall Street Journal*, everyone—even reporters—can be passed off as investment experts. A market crisis—a crash, a correction, or a bear market—will probably cull the ranks of these amateur gurus and may even lead to some lawsuits against media outlets by angry investors who lost their children's college savings by betting on the reporter's advice.

There is a growing trend to make business news entertaining as well as informative. For television, the drive for ratings and resulting advertising dollars has put a premium on pretty faces and increasingly sensational coverage. This creates problems. Separating fact from fluff is difficult, adding to the confusion of the consumer-investor and making it imperative that companies provide context to whatever is being said about them. Companies are also being forced to find more entertaining ways to attract attention while trying to remain credible vehicles for education and information.

In addition, opinion journalism has become an influential subset of business journalism. Opinion, informed or otherwise, is now deamed as newsworthy as the factual information upon which it is based. In fact, opinions have now surpassed facts as the fillers of choice for the growing print space and air time. Call it the business news version of the Monica Lewinsky phenomenon. If there are no more facts to be gleaned from a story and another hour of television air time or page of newsprint to be filled, the goal becomes finding someone who has an opinion on the facts, whether or not that person is qualified to give an opinion. Multiply that by thousands of media outlets, millions of hours of air time, and acres of space, and the mind boggles. It's no wonder the consumer-investor is caught in a credibility vacuum.

The online universe presents its own peculiar pitfalls. Suddenly, anyone with Internet access can call himself a journalist, publishing opinions on all sorts of things for all to see. Chat rooms and bulletin boards have become breeding grounds for rumor and innuendo. Unless detected and squelched, these environments can create serious problems. Online monitoring companies are making a killing watching for discouraging words that are floating through cyberspace. Companies that have been conditioned to fear the power of probing reporters from conventional, influential outlets like *The New York Times* and *The Wall Street Journal* should beware. Research shows that they have much to fear from the burgeoning online universe, where information and misinformation move freely around the world twenty-four hours a day.

How real is this problem? Very, according to Steven Ross, associate professor at the Columbia University Graduate School of Journalism and coauthor of the annual Middleberg/Ross Media in Cyberspace Study. In the world of 24-by-7 online news distribution, according to their 1998 study, "Journalists often got the story wrong, concentrated on breaking news rather than features, and skirted long-standing ethical practices concerning privacy and sourcing." At least established outlets like *The New York Times* and *The Wall Street Journal* make concerted efforts to get the story right. As one *Wall Street Journal* reporter said, "Either it's right, or it doesn't run." Now, any company that has been on the short end of *Journal* exposé would probably disagree. But if the *Journal* and *Times* get the facts wrong, they heed professional ethics and correct their mistakes.

As the head of a small or mid-sized company, you've got an especially big job in dealing with all the upheaval in the business press. Unlike big companies, most of which have in-house corporate communications operations and usually outside public relations help, smaller companies are totally exposed. Few have strategies to take advantage of the growing media universe or protect them from the domino effect the media can trigger if something goes wrong. And therein lies the reason for paying attention to what is going on in the business media.

Consider this theory: Every company—small, medium, and large—has a growth strategy, whether or not it is articulated publicly. Some want to grow to gain more customers and increase market share, maybe even expand globally. Others want to grow to attain the critical mass necessary to acquire a competitor. Still others want to grow to make themselves less delicious as a takeover meal for a bigger competitor. And others want to grow for precisely the opposite reason: to become more attractive as a candidate for a buyout or merger so management can cash out.

Whatever the reason for growth, one component is usually missing from every growth strategy: communications. That's the code word for public relations, and it encompasses any message a company sends to its important audiences, including customers, the media, shareholders, employees, investment analysts, or regulators. Communications are just as important to the successful growth of a company as are manufacturing processes, research and development, the sales force, technology, or any other business unit or function. They will become increasingly important as new business media grow and develop. This is particularly true for small or medium-size companies, which typically are so busy doing what they do, they overlook the fact that they need to tell more investors and customers what they do if they hope to grow. The development of a profile with all key audiences—call it a brand if you want—is just as important for the fledgling company as it is for Microsoft or Ford. Maybe more so.

For growing public companies, especially those fresh out of initial public offerings, a few years into public life, or in an unregulated environment after years of protective restrictions, this is crucial. Suddenly, such a company is not only accountable to its customers and employees, it also must answer to a whole new range of audiences, including shareholders, regulators, and investment analysts. Oh, yes, and the media outlet, which inserts itself into the mix as watchdog, critic, and rating agency. The explosive growth of the media in the United States, coupled with technology, has fostered a convergence of information and opinion. Each audience looks to the others for third-party endorsement about a company.

The point is the good companies understand that a public profile is more than a nice thing to have, a luxury to generate goodwill. It is crucial to growth. Every year, *Fortune* magazine publishes a

list of the most and least admired companies that ties the reputations of companies directly to their financial performance. And
while some critics have questioned the validity of the methodology,
there is no doubt that the way a company is perceived by its key
audience influences the way people react, either as consumers of
the company's products and services or as investors in its stock.
With the growth of the business media, the importance of reputation as a key element of a company's success will continue to grow.
Indeed, success is now a function of consensus among all of a company's key audiences. And the key here is *all* audiences. Companies
can no longer concentrate on one or two audiences such as Wall
Street analysts and their customers.

     The most common mistake companies make is to leave the
media and employees out of the communications mix. The dangers
of ignoring the media are apparent. The dangers of ignoring
employees are less apparent, but many companies are waking up
and doing something to win them over. The old argument is based
on the "two friends" theory: Employees are ambassadors of a company. If they understand and are proud of what their company
stands for, they will tell two friends, who in turn will tell two friends,
and so on. The new argument is more compelling: With the rising
cost of recruiting, training, and retaining qualified employees, especially in technology-intensive industries, it is absolutely crucial to
consider the workforce a key audience and to concentrate on
employees as much as outside audiences.

     It is clear, then, that companies can no longer survive or
grow without paying attention to the media explosion. Indeed, they
have no choice because the media are paying attention to them. To
ignore the trend is dangerous in two ways: First, a company will
receive attention whether it likes it or not, so it might as well be prepared, and second, the opportunities to develop a public profile, a
brand, and consensus among all key audiences are enormous.

     Remember that principle from high school physics: Nature
abhors a vacuum. Consider the news media a vacuum—space on a
page, air time on television and radio, bytes on a computer screen.
If a company does not fill the vacuum with its own story, a reporter

will fill it with his or her own version. And if no facts are available, the vacuum will be filled with speculation. That will immediately put the company on the defensive. A cardinal rule of communications is to help a reporter get the story right the first time rather than correct it if it's wrong—after millions of people have already acted on the misinformation.

In reading the following pages, which explore the phenomenon of the new business media in detail, it is important to remember the driving forces behind it:

▶ *The consumer-investor.* The shift of responsibility to individuals for their future financial well-being has created a new group of Americans who look at companies not simply as makers of products or providers of services but also as potential investments. They seek more information about companies faster and are more comfortable with and reliant upon technology to get it. They want insight, credible opinion, and guidance that will help them make decisions.

▶ *All news, all the time.* To satisfy this new hunger, stories and other information about business instantly circulate around the world, twenty-four hours a day, through all types of media. And consumers of news are capable of and comfortable with getting access to this information in many ways at any time of the day or night, through television, radio, print media, and online channels.

▶ *Business news is entertainment.* The need to entertain as well as inform blurs the line between fact and fluff. To get attention, companies must entertain, too, but they must do so in a way that does not compromise their credibility as sources of education and information.

▶ *Two thumbs up.* In an environment of information overload, the consumer-investor looks to the media for third-party endorsement of their purchasing and investing decisions. Reliance on advertising as a credible medium for information continues to decline.

▶ *Growing pains.* Like any growth industry, the business news media are still building a talent base. With a deficit of qualified journalists schooled in the complexities of business and the pressure to fill more space and air time, the media is highly likely to disseminate incomplete or inaccurate information. And with a deficit of hard facts to fill that space and time, opinion has become the filler of choice.

The objective of this book is not only to help companies understand the dynamics of the new business media environment but also to teach them how to manage it to their advantage. To survive and grow, your company should aim to accomplish the following goals:

▶ *Take control of what you are saying and what is being said about you.*

▶ *Understand your audiences—who they are, what they need to know about your company, how they get their information.*

▶ *Educate as well as inform your audiences.* Tell them not just what you do but what you stand for. Build a reputation for the company and the management.

▶ *Protect your brand in a crisis.* Put some goodwill in the bank.

The success or failure of your company in achieving these goals will have an impact on your sales and stock performance. Companies that fail to understand the very real consequences of the changes in the media universe do so at their peril. The biggest challenge is to develop and manage your identity in what has become a noisy, often chaotic environment. Be patient, be prepared, and be selective. Be as wary of the kid-in-a-candy-store approach as the head-in-the-sand approach. Some exposure is good, but too much can be a problem. Now, more than ever, your company must use the business media to grow, or it will use you.

# CHAPTER 2

# Barbie in the Boardroom

## Business News as Entertainment

S tand-up comic and talk-show host Rosie O'Donnell is embroiled in a heated discussion with one of her guests, actor Tom Selleck, about gun control. She is peppering him with questions and taking him to task for his advocacy for guns. The discussion is taking place on her national television program in the wake of the shootings at a Colorado high school in the spring of 1999. Two students had opened fire on class-mates and teachers, leaving more than a dozen dead and many more wounded. The tragedy, televised live across the country, was watched by shocked but captivated audiences as the drama played out. Horrible scenes of wounded children falling from broken windows and groups of students herded to safety by SWAT teams brandishing automatic weapons quickly became one of the biggest news stories of the year. The tragedy brought renewed calls from Washington for stricter gun controls and rekindled the heated discussion about violence in schools.

The Colorado shootout was not an isolated event. During the preceding two years, similar shootings had occurred in several other schools across the country, though none so bloody or widely publicized. The event also generated criticism of the parents of the children accused of the act for not paying close enough attention to what their children were doing with their free time. What does this have to do with business? Read on.

So heated is the O'Donnell-Selleck discussion and so sensitive is the American public to the problem of violence in schools that other media soon join the frenzy. It is a good story in media terms. Everyone is talking about it. Everyone has an opinion. Following the O'Donnell-Selleck on-air exchange, radio personality Howard Stern goes after O'Donnell for being a hypocrite. His point: How can O'Donnell criticize gun advocates when she is a spokesperson for Kmart, one of the nation's largest retailers of firearms? O'Donnell's holier-than-thou attitude, Stern claims, just doesn't fly.

Nevertheless, Kmart, an unrelated third or fourth party in the discussion, is suddenly thrust into the spotlight. The company has not been linked in any way to the shootings in Colorado, but by virtue of its link with a star, the retailer is in the hot seat. As a large company that serves millions of customers a year, Kmart is no stranger to attention, whether negative or positive. But this is a little different. All of a sudden, Hollywood-based television programs such as "Entertainment Tonight" are talking about Kmart's corporate strategy and merchandise selection. "ET," best known for its reporting on Hollywood's latest romance or cosmetic surgery victim, is talking business, serious business, about a serious, publicly traded company with millions of customers and shareholders. Now, as good as the "ET" reporters are at what they do, Kmart should be squirming. Do these reporters understand the implications of the issue from a business point of view? Do they care? The next thing Kmart's management knows, there are bomb threats against the company's facilities.

If someone had walked into the Kmart boardroom and told its senior executives that the reputation of their company could be at risk because of a strong, albeit peculiar, connection between a television talk show host and comedian, an actor, a radio talk show host, a high school shooting, and a Hollywood gossip television program, that person would have been laughed right out of the room. But there was a risk, and it blew up in Kmart's face. And while it seems like an unlikely situation, it illustrates an important point. In the new media world, business news, like most every other kind of news, has become entertainment. The lines between the traditional areas of coverage—news, weather, sports, business—have been blurred. Weather is news, so much so that it has its own twenty-four-hour cable television station. Sports, particularly with the advent of the $100-million athlete, is also business and entertainment news. In fact, the off-the-field activities of athletes get more news coverage than the games they play. And in a competitive media environment, where television-viewer ratings rule because of their direct relation to a network's ability to generate advertising revenues, personality and glamour have become as important as reporting skills.

## It's Show Business News

On the business news channels, too, it's no longer simply business news; it's *show* business brought to you by real-life Barbies and Kens with flashy sets, toothy smiles, big hair, breathless reports about the day's market activity or the latest merger rumor, and drive-by stock picks from the expert du jour, eager for his or her fifteen minutes of fame. Philip J. Purcell, chairman and chief executive of Morgan Stanley Dean Witter, captured the phenomenon in a recent speech to a securities industry trade group that touched on volatility in the stock market. "The last two weeks have been something," he said. "You know things have gotten out of hand when you turn on the TV at night and see Geraldo Rivera covering the opening of the Hong Kong Stock Exchange."

As John J. Walsh, partner in the Media and First Amendment law firm of Cadwalader, Wickersham and Taft, said in a 1997 speech, "...the purpose of gathering and publishing news

is informing the public, not entertainment, titillation, or vicari-
ous voyeurism—yet today the greater percentage of what is
presented as journalism, at least on the television screen, shares
these characteristics in abundance. Can anything be done about
it?" Probably not.

There are those who would say that a good reporter can
cover any topic, that the same basic skills are adequate for
reporting on a plane crash or a war or a basketball game or a
hostile takeover. But business has its own complexities, and
reporters need a certain amount of grounding to understand
and interpret events properly for readers and viewers. And inter-
pretation is particularly important when it comes to reporting on
publicly held companies in which real people have invested real
money. Bad information or an incorrect assessment of a situation
by an uninformed journalist can be more than simply embarrassing—it can be damaging to a lot of people. Get the score
wrong in a game, and people get annoyed. Forecast a sunny
day, and it rains; people get wet. Report that a company lost five
cents a share last quarter when it earned five cents, and people
could lose money. And losing money is a lot different from getting annoyed or getting wet. The point is that the stakes are
higher when reporting business news, especially in an environment where the consumer-investor is relying on the information
as a basis for decision-making. It is not enough for reporters to
look good. They must also get it right.

## Getting It Right

The transformation of business news into show biz has been
rapid and ragged. In the mid-1980s, when broad-based, serious
business reporting was a fledgling art, the watchword was
demystification. That's when reporters, most of whom had little
business acumen, began to dig deeper into the alien world of
business. They started to cut through corporate jargon and bal-
ance sheets to figure out for readers and viewers the intricacies
of companies' inner workings. It was tough going at first. To

many reporters, financial statements looked as if they had been written in Sanskrit. Annual reports seemed so frighteningly foreign they often sat unopened on reporters' desks. A standing joke among public relations people is that when dealing with the media on a financial story, don't let the reporter do the math. Most reporters, back then anyway, were happy to let someone else do the math. The problem, of course, was that most reporters had liberal arts degrees, not business or finance degrees. They were experts in English or history or political science—some had even gone to journalism school where they had learned the crafts of reporting and editing. But they were by no means experts on business.

Eventually, however, reporters started talking to and writing about the people who ran the companies. They began to associate human faces with Corporate America, linking the personalities of the chief executives to the ways companies did business. It was an educational process for both sides. Reporters gained knowledge about the mysterious world of business, and companies began to see exactly what constituted a business news story. But most of the stories were explanatory, offering little insight. Indeed, there was little demand from readers for insight because they did not have the keen interest in the companies of today's consumer-investor. If a chief executive was a character, with an interesting hobby connected in some way to the business, that was enough. There was even a period in the 1980s when marathon running, from a media standpoint, was the most popular attribute of a chief executive. Newspapers across the country were filled with business feature articles that began, "Frank Lorenzo, head of Eastern Airlines, runs his company the way he runs marathons—fast and hard." These stories were inevitably accompanied by photographs of sweaty senior executives with little body fat looking smug and fit. The message: A fit chief executive means a fit company.

Well, that fad passed, as did the early 1990s' trend of featuring women executives as media stars. In the early days of diversity and political correctness, companies were eager to show that they were promoting women, and the media were eager to report that news. But then, a funny thing happened. Women executives became newsworthy because they were women and not because of the company they owned or worked for or their job performance. I remember a news meeting at *The New York Times* in the early 1990s at which a number of editors had gathered to review a list of stories for the Sunday business section. Among the offerings was a feature about a woman business executive of a large company. As is the practice in these meetings, each editor presents a case for his or her story lineup, giving details about the interesting points. As one editor pitched the story about the woman executive, it became clear that beyond the fact that the subject of the story was a woman, there wasn't much meat to the proposed piece. A senior editor in charge of selecting the story lineup, herself a woman, interrupted. "At the risk of sounding politically incorrect," she said with a smile, "I think we are probably past the point where a person's gender is the determining factor in whether or not they are newsworthy. At least I hope we are." The story died, and in that small exchange we all learned an important lesson. The demands of readers were changing. The editor touting the story had seized on the personality aspect of business, and we had not seen a problem with that until the senior editor spoke her mind. In short, writing a personality story was easier than doing the math.

The few who had some training in business and finance or who had gone out of their way to learn a few tricks, tried their hand at analysis. They looked at issues such as vision, leadership, and management theory, though in the early days many editors considered that kind of thinking to be way ahead of the curve. And, frankly, there simply wasn't widespread demand for that kind of in-depth reporting on business.

Most of these developments occurred in the print media. The few business stories that made it to television were very consumer oriented—retail sales at Christmas, the most popular toys, the most dangerous toys, the price of gas, airline fares, cola wars, burger wars, and the like. These types of sto-ries did not really look behind the news, into the financial issues of companies or the intricacies of their operations. Tele-vision didn't allow the time for in-depth reporting. A minute-long report could hardly explain much more than the top line of a story. And, more important, it didn't need to. Consumers didn't care about anything beyond their personal links to the companies in question—namely, the products and services they bought. The business of business was pretty boring to the average person. A company's annual shareholders' meeting, for example, certainly did not make great visuals for televi-sion.

## Enter Hollywood

Then the movie "Wall Street" came along as a startling example of the way Hollywood can bring the dead to life. Rarely, if ever, do such shareholders' gatherings have the drama of corporate raider Gordon Gekko's famous "Greed is good" speech at the annual meeting of a fictional paper company. As angry stockholders cheer him on, Gekko criti-cizes the rows of sheepish vice presidents in attendance for the high salaries and costly perks they receive. As unrealistic as its depiction of these annual powwows was, that movie did much to glamorize the world of business, particularly Wall Street. It was portrayed as a game of big money and big risks. The game was exciting, exhilarating, and sometimes scary.

The movie did much to generate interest in business among an entire population of Americans who had never before cared about it. All of a sudden, business was sexy, intriguing, cool. Average people from working class families like Bud Fox, the character played by Charlie Sheen in "Wall Street," could make lots of money by playing the stock mar-ket. If there were people around like Gordon Gekko, who on the surface passed himself off as a champion of shareholders' rights, companies would have to be accountable for their actions. It was a different way to capture the American dream—invest in a company, then sit back and watch the money grow. This business stuff is pretty slick after all, the movie told the millions of Americans who saw it. And today, the news media, particularly television, try to recapture that spirit in their coverage.

With a media audience hungry for entertainment and information in the same package, and technology that allows delivery of both from around the world, it was inevitable that business news would make the transition to a business where reporters are personalities. The television examples are the most obvious: Lou Dobbs, the modern guru of television business news who has started an Internet venture, has found ways to extend his influential "CNN Moneyline" persona. "CNN Moneyline News Hour," combines business and news coverage. While Dobbs did not report on weather and sports, he took on a personality beyond the anchor desk. In advertisements for his "Business Unusual" news feature program, he jumped out of a helicopter in a wetsuit into the ocean. Maria Bartiromo, the rapid-fire CNBC reporter who delivers stand-up commentary amid the trading-floor chaos at the New York Stock Exchange, has been nicknamed "the money honey" by both admirers and critics. She has become one of the most-watched anchors in business news, appealing to the male-dominated Wall Street culture that likes a little sex appeal with its financial news. When she lost her anchor position on CNBC's evening Business Center program in mid-1999, the move was fodder for coverage by the tabloid newspapers, which treated her as if she were a big-time celebrity. Neil Cavuto, probably one of the hardest working anchors, brings a chatty style, a sense of humor, and in-depth homework to his late afternoon business show, "The Cavuto Business Report," on Fox News. And Suzie Gharib and Paul Kangas provide a high-energy, no-nonsense rap on "PBS Nightly Business Report," the top-rated business show in the United States. With anchor personalities like these, Louis Rukeyser, the granddaddy of television business news, looks positively archaic on the set of the PBS staple "Wall Street Week."As host, he offers quirky, homespun investment wisdom from an armchair.

Even traditional print media are getting into the act. Reporters from *The Wall Street Journal, The New York Times, Fortune,* and other old-line business publications now appear regularly on television. They give reports on stories they are following and, in effect, are scooping their own publications. Many print reporters, including those from *The Wall Street Journal*, report regularly on national radio as well. This phenomenon is not nearly as astounding as the questions raised by the fact that journalists are interviewing other journalists. Why aren't the interviewers doing their own reporting? Or has the world run so short on experts that reporters have to interview other reporters? And what does it say about competition, the real driver in the newsgathering business, when reporters who would have been fierce rivals in days gone by are freely giving each other information with a smile?

Suffice it to say that in its formative years, business news has fallen prey to the same trap as other news: The need to fill time and space has generated this absurd practice. America saw it throughout coverage of President Clinton's scandalous affair with Intern Monica Lewinsky, which led to impeachment hearings. Political commentators, who had run out of sources with real information to convey, were interviewing other political commentators, over and over and over again. Reporters were interviewing other reporters. News anchors were interviewing each other. Opinion, rumor, and speculation quickly overtook facts as the meat of newscasts. As Philip Purcell of Morgan Stanley Dean Witter said, things had gotten out of hand.

By the way, with few exceptions, it is easy to distinguish the print journalists from the professional television reporters. Most print reporters, unaccustomed to looking at anything brighter than the letters on their computer screens, squint uncomfortably into the television lights. They mumble, they stutter. They do not have decent haircuts, professional makeup, or tailored clothing. They are neither Barbies nor Kens. They are, for the most part, not the kind of television personalities who would constitute entertainment by today's standards. But by virtue of the media outlets they represent, they bring instant credibility to a television audience seeking reliable third-party sources.

## The Need to Fill Time and Space

Those who do not report on the stories themselves talk about the news organizations that do the reporting. Michael Bloomberg, the founder of the ever-expanding Bloomberg financial information empire, has become almost as ubiquitous as his computer terminals. He is everywhere promoting his company, which has revolutionized business news by covering virtually every story in every corner of the world and delivering it to the desk tops of thousands of subscribers to his service.

Michael Bloomberg's presence is an interesting lesson in the personification of business news and a powerful competitive tool for his company. Respected as a successful Wall Street player before he entered the world of news and information, Bloomberg has the credibility and insight the consumer-investor wants. He does not pretend to be a journalist or a technical expert. But he has the money to hire top journalists and technicians to deliver information quickly and in a format that subscribers find convenient and useful. His personal endorsements set him apart from major competitors—the respected but faceless news organizations such as Reuters, Dow Jones, Bridge News, and The Associated Press. Bloomberg knows that many people like to see and know the person behind the company with which they are doing business. He is not shy about making himself available anywhere all of the time. It is powerful brand reinforcement for subscribers to Bloomberg's service to regularly see and hear the man whose name is on the machine they use to get stock quotes, sports scores, and the weather.

Another newcomer to the business media scene is the journalist/business owner. James Cramer, for example, is an investment professional, columnist, and founder of TheStreet.com, an online business newswire. While he has come under fire from some conventional media for what they say is a conflict of interest from running a business about which he writes as a journalist, he continues to write, own, and promote his ventures on television, in print, and online. A colorful speaker and prolific writer, Cramer is a regular guest on CNBC, where he offers commentary on just about anything that comes his way—including frequent claims that his wife has a much better understanding of the financial markets than he does. His quirky style makes viewers want to watch this dynamic personality just a few minutes longer. The fact that his methods have not offended those who consume his extraordinary output of information and opinion says much about the tolerance and sensitivities of audiences in this new media environment. Cramer's readers and viewers apparently care less about any ethical tightrope walking he may do than about the value of the information he provides. In a world hungry for information, Cramer's frequent appearances on television and in print seem to be enough of a stamp of credibility to keep his customers coming back for more.

Mainstream media, too, have discovered that their audiences like a splash of business news now and then. Charlie Rose, the thoughtful PBS talk show host of "The Charlie Rose Show" and "60 Minutes II" reporter, who is best known for interviewing celebrity entertainers, writers, and other mainstream personalities, is devoting more time to financial matters. Stock market corrections have become the subject of panel discussions in Rose's Park Avenue studios, which happen to be located in Michael Bloomberg's main New York news bureau space. Rose is even tackling some of the larger economic issues facing the country, such as Social Security reform. Something strange is happening when the guest list for a single Charlie Rose Show includes comic Joan Rivers, novelist Garrison Keillor, and the chairman of a Wall Street brokerage house.

And then there's the online universe. The Wall Street Journal Interactive Edition, TheStreet.com, CBSMarketWatch, SmartMoney.com, Business Week Online lead the parade. While none is as personality driven as The Drudge Report or Motley Fool, the trend is in that direction. In fact, James Cramer of TheStreet.com has used the online world in conjunction with television and print to reach the guru status of a Matt Drudge, the online television political commentator.

What's the upshot of business news as show business news for the consumer-investor and the companies that serve them? It's that substantive news is easily lost beneath the glitz. The fast-paced, splashy approach is distracting. The average consumer of this information generally has difficulty separating fact from fluff. And the rise of opinion journalism has blurred the line between fact and speculation. The motives of many commentators are unclear. Do they have a vested interest in what they are discussing or is their opinion truly independent and unbiased? Doesn't someone like James Cramer have to separate his agenda as journalist from his agenda as businessman to ensure credibility in both arenas? These questions remain unanswered. In fact, with business news happening so quickly, there are new questions and concerns arising almost daily. The consumer-investor is left in a credibility vacuum, wondering whom to believe and whom to dismiss.

## The CEO Star

The new media maelstrom is a big problem your company has to solve. In a news environment driven by personalities and entertainment value, in which the lines of credibility are blurred, companies now must have believable but also entertaining people to do the talking for them. If your company's spokespeople interview well on television, chances are they will be asked to perform again. Over time, they may also be asked to comment on issues that are not specific to your company, such as industry trends, economic events, even politics. When your spokespeople are cultivated as experts on topics other than what your company does, that is a sure sign they are on the road to guru status.

Is this good or bad for your company? It's good in that a spokesperson who is asked to comment on broad issues is perceived to be a thought leader. This person is elevated beyond the realm of someone who knows how to run a company to the level of someone who has a grasp of the big picture, someone with vision, insight, even knowledge. And by association, this visionary's company is perceived to be a thought-leader that cultivates such lofty thinking.

The trickle-down to the consumer-investor can be effective for your company. A company that is perceived as thinking well probably has more of that thinking in its products and services than a company that does not think well. So the consumer side of the consumer-investor has a little more perspective when making a purchasing decision. Chances are, consumers will buy products and services they perceive to be well thought out, not simply well presented. In other words, consumers equate a thinking company with products that will last a long time and be useful in the long term as well.

In addition, a company that is not only involved in thinking about the big picture but is also asked to share its thoughts with the world must have some idea about what's going on and what's coming next. Logic would dictate that such a company is a good bet as an investment. After all, while the historical performance of stock is a good benchmark, it is just that—history. Law requires that investment companies include a disclaimer in their marketing information that reminds people that the historical performance of a company's stock is not a guarantee of future performance. For the investor side of the consumer-investor, what lies ahead for a company is far more important when determining future investment needs.

So becoming a personality is good, right? Isn't the new media environment ready-made for "the CEO star," the chatty, charming senior executive who looks good and is comfortable on camera? Not necessarily. There is a danger that companies will fall into the same credibility trap in which business news finds itself through overexposure. Companies must make sure their spokespeople comment only on issues relevant to the company and only in media outlets that are strategically important to the audiences a company wants to reach. Here's an extreme, but illustrative, example: If your company makes airplane engine parts, there is probably not much benefit in having the chief executive officer accept an invitation to appear on MTV.

## Selecting and Positioning the Spokesperson

Companies must also make sure they are using the right people to talk about the right things. Such a practice not only keeps executives from becoming burned out and overexposed, it also protects them from commenting on areas about which they have limited knowledge and from embarrassing themselves in front of important audiences. For example, it should be appropriate for a chief executive officer to comment publicly on the quarterly financial results of the company, but a discussion about a new employee training program or the expansion of a remote plant is best left to those who are in charge of the project.

Companies should beware of allowing senior staff to speak on behalf of the industry especially if the story is a dangerous one. If the company is not involved with the issue, it is not smart public relations to be held up as an apologist for the industry or competitors—even if the spokesperson is a charming personality with lots of experience talking to teh media. For example, if your company is an Internet server, you do not want your staff commenting on a service interruption at America Online.

It is important to remember that a company's audience expects to hear certain things from certain people. In the same way it would sound peculiar for a professional athlete to be interviewed on American military strategy, an interview with a company's chief executive officer about the hiring of a junior-level sales associate would have audiences scratching their heads and wondering why. Spokespeople and their messages should be matched with the expectations of the audience.

There are broad but distinct categories of subjects about which various spokespersons should comment:

> ▶ *A chief executive officer usually talks about corporate strategy and outlook, philosophy, and vision; industry and competitive issues; and any macro trends that may influence the performance of the company.* The rule of thumb is to establish the chief executive as the ultimate visionary for the company and the environment in which it does business.

> ▶ *A president or chief operating officer usually discusses the company's operations including structural changes and initiatives, major personnel moves, or business wins.* The goal is to establish these spokespeople as the generals in the day-to-day battles, fully aware of the company, the competitors, and the business environment.

> ▶ *A chief financial officer, if he or she speaks at all, should stick to the numbers.* The average CFO is usually not the most effective spokesperson, even if the audience is exclusively a group of investment analysts. This executive should take a supporting role to the chief executive officer and president in any public discussions.

> ▶ *A unit manager or other professional usually discusses the products and services that are specific to that unit.* If properly trained, the unit manager should be able to link the company's products and services directly to its overall strategy, and talk about what he or she makes or does and how important it is to the growth of the company.

Companies eager for exposure must also be wary of invitations to participate in media interviews or other forums in which they may be used as examples of how not to do something. A couple years ago, amid the buzz about technology and online trading, Reuters, the big London-based media and financial information company, sponsored a panel in New York discussing the ways technology was changing the landscape of Wall Street. On one side of the panel were representatives from the new technology firms such as discount brokerage houses, online trading firms, and technology experts—the nerds. On the other side were representatives of several large, old-line full-service stock brokerage houses—the suits. In the audience were dozens of reporters eager to watch the action. It soon became clear that the agenda and the line of questioning were slanted in favor of the nerds. The reporters relished the spectacle of the suits squirming in their seats when asked questions about what their firms were doing to stem the onslaught of high-tech whiz kids who were cutting into their business. It was truly good theater and therefore good copy.

It was clear from the start that the suits had been set up. And while most of them performed well, giving credible defenses to the charge that they were slow-moving dinosaurs, they were obviously in danger of being embarrassed. Should they have been surprised to have been put on the defensive? Not really, when you consider that the event was sponsored by a company that is not only a provider of technology to the financial services industry and a big player in the development of online trading systems, but also a global provider of business news and information. Reuters got twice the bang for its buck.

The lessons are clear: Know the agenda of the interview or event, determine if it is in your company's best strategic interest to participate, then accept or decline as you see fit. Resist the temptation to go for the sure hit if it does not have clear and overwhelming strategic benefit. Ask yourself, Does it get your key messages to your key audiences? Remember, when it comes to dealing with the media, discretion is the better part of valor. There is no shame in saying no. In fact, companies new to the media relations arena should say no more often, even though the lure of stardom is seductive.

## Summary of Trends

▶ *It's not business news.* It's *show* business news. In a world hungry for entertainment and information, business news has become a personality business.

▶ *Looking good and getting it right.* A downside of the glitz is that glamour often outshines the need for reporters and news anchors to understand the intricacies of business. Misinformation or misinterpretation from an uninformed journalist can be more than embarrassing—it can hurt the company and those who have money invested in it.

▶ *Traditional media in the spotlight.* The need to fill space has prompted former reporting rivals to become allies, trading information freely and raising competitive issues about news gathering.

▶ *The rise of opinion journalism.* When the facts run out, opinion fills in. The problem lies in the dubious quality of the opinions expressed and the credentials of those who give them. The consumer-investor is caught in a credibility vacuum.

▶ *The many faces of business news.* The demand for information about companies has business news popping up where it is least expected. And the traditional rules of journalism, including sourcing and conflict of interest, have become secondary to churning out vast amounts of information.

## Lessons for Companies

▶ *Entertain, educate, and inform.* To get attention, companies need to entertain, too. But they have to find ways to do it that do not compromise their credibility as sources of information for the consumer-investor.

▶ *The rise of the "CEO star."* The rise of personality-driven business news has created corporate media darlings. The good news is that if CEO stars are well managed, they can be assets. The bad news is that if they are mismanaged, they can damage a company's reputation.

▶ *The halo effect of thought leadership.* A company spokesperson who is sought after by the media for opinions can make the company look good by association. If a company's chief spokesperson is a thought leader, the company must be one, too.

▶ *The pitfalls of stardom.* Overexposure is like the curiosity that killed the cat. Companies need to make sure that in their quest to make their spokespeople entertaining personalities, they remember that the quality and benefit of an opportunity is as important as the exposure itself.

# CHAPTER 3

# The Dumbing Down of News

## A Talent Deficit Grows

D uring the late 1990s, as consolidation spread through the financial services industry, almost every company was considered to be in play, at least by the media. It didn't matter how big or small a company was, or how vehemently its senior management vowed publicly to stay independent. Reporters who covered banks, brokerage firms, mutual fund companies, and insurers played a regular game of linking two companies together and finding a financial analyst who thought such combinations might make sense. It was a peculiar exercise in pulling names from a hat, stitching them together, and seeing if the resulting combination had any validity. *The Wall Street Journal* became skilled at the game, and other media outlets soon followed. Inevitably, articles appeared linking firms that were based on little more than speculation. Among the most spectacular of these fictional combinations was Chase Manhattan and Merrill Lynch.

The problem, of course, was that it was a case of the blind leading the blind. Armed with unsubstantiated speculation, reporters would write stories and their publications would print them—or their broadcast outlets would air them. In a frenzy, reporters who had not taken the time to consult their own Ouija boards or merger gurus followed with their own articles, based on similarly flimsy speculation or none at all. The fact that the rumor had appeared somewhere else provided good enough reason and ample enough credibility to recycle it. It was a case of if everybody says it, it must be true. And the editors or producers who are supposed to be the guardians of media integrity didn't seem to care. Where were the voices of reason who would say to their charges that if you can't confirm the rumor with evidence, it is simply a rumor and therefore not a real news story? Where was the time-honored credo of responsible journalism that a story is not complete without at least two and preferably three reliable sources—and reliable meaning people who know what's going on because they are involved, not some person who when asked said a particular combination of companies would be interesting? And did any of these editors or producers think it important to remind their scribes that these were public companies about which they were writing, companies in which real people had real money invested, and that the dangers of being wrong were costlier than if they were writing about the weather?

## The Rumor Mill Frenzy

The disturbing consequenes of playing the Wall Street rumor mill on the pages of America's newspapers were ignored in the frenzy to match competitors. At the risk of being left behind, the media threw out the accepted rules of journalistic conduct and care. And all across the country, and indeed around the world, young reporters would simply be told to match competitors' stories. They had to find their own sources and ask them what they thought about this combination of companies or that one. If they couldn't match the competition, they were told to write articles quoting the competition. If I had a dime for every newswire and online merger article that included the phrase, "*The Wall Street Journal* reported today that..." I'd be rich.

As the corporate spokesman for PaineWebber, I was constantly beseiged by telephone calls from reporters, many of
whom barely knew what PaineWebber did and cared only that
someone somewhere had said the firm was a takeover target. For
those like me—Wall Street spokespeople—the takeover rumor
mill was not only annoying but also dangerous. PaineWebber was
a favorite target for several reasons—it was not too big and not
too small. It would, according to the rumors, make a tasty meal
for a larger bank or brokerage firm but would not cost too much
to buy. In addition, it was one of only two independent national
full-service brokerage firms left on Wall Street, the other being
Merrill Lynch. That meant, presumably, it would be a cleaner play
for an acquirer—the firm would not have to be pried loose from a
parent, partner, or third party.

For about eighteen months, from early 1997 to late
1998, the media paired PaineWebber with almost every financial institution, foreign and domestic, from Dresdner Bank
and Deutschebank to Bank of America, Chase Manhattan,
First Union, Lehman Brothers, Prudential Securities, and Gold-
man, Sachs. The run began in March 1997 when *Business
Week* published an article saying that the chairman of
PaineWebber had been in talks with the chairman of Bank of
America about combining the two institutions. Despite the
fact that when the reporter called to ask he was told that no
such meeting had taken place—indeed, the two men had
never even met socially—he wrote the article anyway, quoting an unnamed but "reliable" source. The fact that this
reporter is no novice in the business points up an important
point: Youth and inexperience are not the only recipe for
trouble.

For the next year and a half, PaineWebber was reported to
have been in talks with a dozen or more potential partners,
despite the fact that the firm had been independent for almost
120 years and had said repeatedly in public that it intended to
remain that way. In fact, the company went beyond that, saying
that its real goal was to acquire smaller businesses that enhanced

its core strengths, rather than to be acquired. So, not only did PaineWebber have a strong stance against being acquired, it made a public, for-the-record declaration that it was hungry to acquire. In an ironic twist, a reporter for *The Wall Street Journal* inquired at one point about writing a story on the number of rumors that had swirled around PaineWebber, with the angle that where there's smoke there's fire.

For some unknown reason, the rumors usually began on Friday afternoons, and for the next ninety minutes my phones would light up like Christmas trees. On certain days, we would log upwards of two hundred  calls in a sixty- to ninety-minute period—about three calls a minute—from frantic reporters seeking confirmation or denial of the latest rumor. During that period, the firm's stock would be very volatile, and the stock exchanges would ask as a matter of course if there were any corporate developments that might explain the activity. Our policy was not to comment on rumors or speculation, in that even a "no comment" floated out in such a feeding frenzy could be construed as an indication that the company had something to hide. Though no one could ever confirm it, there was widespread speculation on Wall Street that the people generating such rumors were skilled stock manipulators trying to make a few bucks.

This frenzy became so routine that our group would prepare for it every Friday at about lunch time. Senior executives would call regularly mid-afternoon to ask about the rumor of the day. As the firm's chairman was fond of telling reporters, in an effort to quell the rumors: "In the 1980s, when the auto makers were getting into the financial services industry, one rumor was that we were being taken over by Ford. But I drove a Chrysler, so that would never have worked. No one ever bothered to ask me what kind of car I drove." Most of the reporters, scribbling away frantically and hoping for a connection between past and present, missed the point of the story. What he was trying to say was check your sources. Don't be so quick to report stories that cannot be substantiated. It's not just irresponsible, it can have a serious impact on the companies involved and the people who invest in them.

## The Talent Deficit

For the reporters, the point was lost. But for companies seeking to understand the business media, the point is an important one. Like any industry that experiences rapid, explosive growth, the business news media are suffering a talent deficit. In an effort to produce content for newspapers, wire services, magazines, television and radio programs, and online services, news organizations are recruiting faster, training less, and moving younger, inexperienced reporters into the often complicated world of dollars and deals. The overall effect is a lowering of standards across the board—a dangerous environment for information about your company to be floating around in unchecked.

At the same time, the consumer-investor is looking to the media for more in-depth perspective. This group wants someone who can help them wade through the mountains of information available and help them form opinions that will lead to purchasing and investment decisions. Remember Siskel and Ebert? The pressure is on the media not only to report but also to advise. And therein lies the biggest danger of the talent deficit. Journalists, experienced and novice, are being forced to try their hands at giving investment advice. The liability for the reporters and the news outlets for which they work is worrisome. Yet, the practice is becoming more common, not less. For those greenhorns who are still trying to figure out price-to-earnings ratios, providing investment advice is simply ludicrous.

There is even a move by some media outlets to hire investment analysts as reporters or columnists, though it is pretty difficult for even the most prestigious media outlets to match the financial compensation that Wall Street firms pay analysts, even the young ones. Still, a number of youthful analysts have made the jump and are trying their hands at journalism. But as any journalist will tell you, the world of journalism is not the world of research analysis. Different responsibilities and motivations go along with being a member of the media. And while the skills used by a reporter and an analyst to gather and process information may be similar, the angle on the finished product is quite different. The hybrid journalist-analyst has yet to set the business media world on fire.

It is important to note, too, that all of this has occurred in the unprecedented bull market of the mid- to late 1990s. At a time when the Dow Jones industrial average rose from 3,000 to 11,000, anyone who picked stocks by throwing darts at *The Wall Street Journal* stock tables had a pretty good chance of beating the S&P 500. So, the euphoria and resulting feeling of indestructibility fostered by the bull's run has made everyone an expert—even the reporter a year or two out of journalism school or the analyst who turned reporter just last week. The false sense that playing the stock market is easy and returns are guaranteed creates an underlying disaster waiting to happen to a generation of investors who have not seen a market crash, severe correction, or extended bear market. Research by PaineWebber and The Gallup Organization, published in PaineWebber "Index of Investor Optimism" (1999), has shown that investors, particularly younger investors, have extraordinarily high expectations for annual returns on their investments in the equity markets, an optimism clearly born of inexperience. While a catastrophe may curb the unbridled practice of the media-dispensing investment advice, it is likely that the consumer-investor's appetite for information will increase, not decrease, in times of trouble. So the cycle will continue, though perhaps in a slightly different form.

Companies need to be wary of this trend. Do you really want journalists, particularly inexperienced ones, offering advice to investors about your company? In the new media environment, you may have no choice. But you do have a choice about helping the media give informed advice. This goes back to the need to tell the world what your company is really all about.

The talent deficit is not the reporters' fault. When thrust into new situations that require some background knowledge, they can't help but make some mistakes. Remember when Bill Clinton was running for president the first time and one of his strategies was to capture the youth vote by making appearances on MTV? During one interview, a young host asked the candidate what musical influences he liked. Clinton's reply, "Thelonius Monk," drew a blank stare from the twentysomething interviewer "Who was the loneliest monk?" she asked.

Add to this the competitive pressures this environment brings, and you have a breeding ground of errors. In an effort to get the story in a hurry, reporters are likely to get it wrong. In some online news services, reporters and editors have no choice—their computer systems are programmed to post a story online after a certain amount of time, whether the information has been checked or not.

## Promotional Agendas

Competition is also driving some media outlets to change long-held standards of fairness. And increasingly, marketing and promotional agendas are driving editorial decisions and, in some cases, jeopardizing editorial integrity. An example: *Business Week* had been working on an article about an investment broker who had been participating in unauthorized seminars in the Caribbean that offered tax advice to Americans wanting to move assets off-shore. While it was unclear whether the advice was running afoul of tax laws, there was no question that this broker had not obtained the necessary approval to participate in the seminar. (Most major Wall Street firms have strict policies governing such activities.) And while the firm had dismissed the broker upon learning of the practice, the reporter considered the tale interesting enough to constitute a story. The good news was that I as the spokesman for the firm in question, PaineWebber, knew the reporter well and had worked with her for many years. She was consistently straightforward and up-front when writing something potentially negative about the firm. This was one of those cases that she was bound to write about despite agreeing that the company had acted appropriately and responsibly in dismissing the offender. However, she said, the article would not be large and it would appear near the back of the magazine as an interesting, though not prominent, piece. For us, that was the only silver lining to an otherwise gray cloud. In a company such as PaineWebber that employs nearly 20,000 people, you get a few bad apples. It is an occupational hazard. And this was such an obscure occurrence with such limited interest we believed few other media would pick up the story, and those that did would probably not give it significant play. Still, we battened down the hatches and prepared standby statements in case other reporters called.

Now, with the advent of the Internet as a source of news, PaineWebber had become accustomed to looking for postings of articles to newspaper and magazine Web sites in advance of the actual hard copies becoming available on newsstands or to subscribers. The contents of *Business Week*, for example, appeared on its Web site every Thursday night. For those who asked the magazine's promotions department, an advance copy of the magazine could be picked up at the security desk of its Sixth Avenue office building in Manhattan any time after 5:15 P.M. on Thursdays. So on the day the negative article about the investment broker was to be published, we had all the bases covered. We had dutifully spoken with our contacts at *Business Week's* promotions department, and a copy was waiting for us at the appointed time and place. We were also ready to tune in to the Web site sometime around 6 P.M. to see the story there.

Then, something peculiar happened. At about 1:30 P.M. on the Thursday the article was to appear, I received a call from a reporter at Bloomberg, and a few minutes later, from one at the Dow Jones News Service. Did I have a comment, they asked, on the *Business Week* story about the broker and the tax seminars in the Caribbean? I was dumbfounded, and I told them so. I knew the article had been written, but I had not seen it. In fact, it was not supposed to be public for another four or five hours. My friend, the Bloomberg reporter, laughed. "You got PR-ed," she said. "The story's not out, but they put out a press release about it." Sure enough, on the news wires was a three-paragraph promotional release synopsizing the article. PaineWebber was mentioned prominently, and the intimation was that something very bad was happening at the firm.

In its eagerness to promote itself, *Business Week* had put us in a position of being asked to comment about an article we had not seen. And the wire services, which would write probably only one story on the issue based on the press release, would be able to include only a "no comment" from us because it would have been imprudent and foolish to provide a statement in the dark.

This shotgun approach angered a number of people at PaineWebber and *Business Week*. The reporter, when told of the situation, was livid, particularly because we had been accommodating and helpful throughout her research. She agreed that the situation had been handled badly by the people at her end and that her relationship with us had been strained because of the overeagerness of the marketing people. In response, I wrote a letter to *Business Week's* senior editors expressing the firm's disappointment with the way the matter had been handled. It was, I suggested, unprofessional conduct in that it did not allow a major publicly traded company the opportunity to properly respond to questions about a potentially damaging issue. Such a stunt would be expected from a lesser media light, but *Business Week* should know better and act better. I never received a response.

For companies, the talent deficit of the new business media has pros and cons. While the less experienced journalists may be more pliable than the veteran reporters, they are also more prone to mistakes or misinterpretations based on lack of industry knowledge and training. It is in companies' best interests to educate as well as inform. This is particularly true for companies whose names are not yet household names. While most everyone knows what Ford Motor Company does, the general public know nothing about thousands of small and midsize companies. The process of reaching the public is, of necessity, an exercise in schooling reporters, and can lead to excellent relationships with reporters as they become more seasoned.

## Educating the Audience

Companies must understand that a big part of developing a profile is educating their key audiences. Your company can do that by helping viewers or readers understand your perspective. In every news story in good papers there is something called the perspective paragraph or, in shorthand, the "nut graf." It is the paragraph near the beginning of the story, that puts into context the event that generated the news story in the first place. For example, if the lead paragraph says, "ABC Company announced today that it will buy XYZ Company for $500 million," the nut graf would read something like this: "The acquisition is key to the growth strategy of ABC company, which for the last two years has been setting its course to become a global leader in widget technology. With the addition of XYZ's manufacturing operations in Europe and the Far East, ABC has taken a big step toward that goal."

If your company can add to that a favorable comment from an analyst as an independent third party endorsement, then you have accomplished a lot. And a reader will know what has happened and why and will get a second opinion from an expert about it. All that information will help shape the reader's opinion and may influence a decisive action to buy your product, buy your stock, or even apply for a job at your firm. Or the reader may simply decide to start paying attention to what you're doing, to see if you might be a company with which to do business or invest in at some point. If nothing else, the reader will think of you and may talk to friends about you. The kind of word-of-mouth exposure that comes from the question "What do you know about ABC Company?" is priceless. If the perspective is not there, or if reporters don't know it's there, the deal is simply an isolated incident that says nothing about the company except that it has $500 million to spend. And in an age of multibillion-dollar deals, such a transaction would not create a big media bang. When I was an editor at *The New York Times* in the mid-1990s, deals of hundreds of millions of dollars were lucky to make it into the Company News briefs. Even billion-dollar deals became a dime a dozen, and only an extraordinary set of circumstances or a recognizable brand name would give them a chance to merit a full-sized story.

The need to educate is especially important if your company has no brand name or a brand name that is not widely known. It is essential that you take the time to explain to reporters in minute detail what your company does and why, and where it fits in the grand scheme of the industry. The problem: Many company people simply don't want to take the time to do this. They get impatient. Some even get mad. One executive with whom I worked would get so angry with reporters who did not understand the intricacies of advanced accounting principles that media relations contact was a liability, not a benefit. Perfectly benign informational interviews with reporters would turn into shouting matches and set back by several steps the goodwill the company had built with the reporter. Once I found out about this bad habit of his, the executive was never put in front of the media again.

In the campaign to get the story out, however, beware of running up against a solid reporter who knows his or her stuff. After reading the preceding accounts, you may think no such reporter exists. But the major outlets are full of very sharp journalists mixed in with the rank novices who know a lot about you and your company—or they know how to find out in a hurry—and they can tell when you're trying to use them to promote your company's agenda. In such cases, the effort to "spin" the story with the reporter can backfire.

An example: In the early 1990s, a major European airline was in a bitter squabble with its American partner over ownership and management issues. The problems threatened to break apart the partnership, which had been forged under and held up as an example of the value of the Open Skies Agreement that allowed reservations, flight and fare links between U.S. and foreign carriers. Because of this, the conflict between the two was magnified, and the outcome was watched as a harbinger for all other such partnerships. Media scrutiny was intense and emotions were running high on all sides.

Fueling the fire was the fact that the American carrier was headed by a flamboyant chairman who was a real pro at playing the media. He was smart and outrageous, a powerful combination that even the most responsible reporters couldn't ignore. By contrast, the Europeans were staid, soft spoken, and subtle in their approach. They were no less tenacious or committed to an agenda than their American counterpart; they simply had a different style of dealing with the media.

My firm represented the Europeans, and the account manager believed that we could use their low-key approach to our advantage with the major, responsible media outlets such as *The New York Times* and *The Wall Street Journal*. Despite warnings from our media team, including me, that it would be difficult to "spin" reporters at these outlets, the account manager advised the client that we would arrange such interviews. We were committed, and we offered the *Times* two of the senior executives of the European airline to tell their side of the story. The representatives performed as expected. The reporter, a specialist in the airline industry, had followed the issue and was grateful for the opportunity to interview the senior decision-makers.

The account manager was ecstatic. Not only did he look smart with his client for hooking the company up with a reporter from *The New York Times,* he boldly proclaimed the *Times* would write a glowing article that would expose the American partner as a liar and the Europeans would, by virtue of public support, win the day. His enthusiasm, naïve at the least, dangerously overin-flated the expectations of the client. In the end, his promise did not come true. The next day's paper was void of any article as was the following day's paper. The account manager couldn't under-stand. He wanted to talk to the reporter. So we arranged a confer-ence call during which he asked why there had been no coverage. The response from the reporter was simple and to the point: "Don't fight your battle through me." He went on to explain, without any malice, that his job was not to become the conduit for a "he said, he said" exchange between our client and its Amer-ican partner. His job, the reporter patiently explained, was to offer perspective on the issue and present both sides evenly and equally. The account manager didn't get it. That day, yet another PR man learned that spin doesn't work the way it used to, especially with reporters who are knowledgeable about the industries they cover.

The point is that there is a line between being educational and being transparent in pushing your agenda. It may be eas-ier to do both with inexperienced reporters, whose eagerness to learn may blind them, at least temporarily, to your motives. But it's O.K. to try. After all, the media push their agendas on the companies they cover, so pushing back a little is perfectly acceptable. Just know whom you're pushing. From time to time, especially as your company grows in prominence, you will bump up against top flight journalists who have seen all the tricks and won't bite. It may startle you at first, especially if you have been wading your way through the weak talent pool of other media. There will be no harm done. When you're pushing your point of view and it meets with skepticism, don't get mad. You can't control the minds of very experienced jour-nalists. Just make yourself available to them when they want to talk to you, and start building relationships with them.

## Reporters Are People, Too

And one more important point about the talent deficit in the media. Never forget that despite what your experience may tell you, reporters are people, too. They are prone to the same human emotions and influenced by the same forces of human nature as the rest of us. A lot of people in companies forget that, and they miss wonderful opportunities to build great relationships with reporters, especially inexperienced ones. If you understand that these people are under immense pressure to produce on deadline in a highly charged, competitive environment, you will realize that they are happy to hear a friendly, helpful voice on the other end of the line. Through the tough talk and bluster, a lot of these kids are scared stiff. Scared that they will get something wrong, scared that they'll get beaten on a story, and scared that they'll lose their jobs. Believe me, I've been there, lying awake in my bed at 3 A.M. wondering what the competition had that I didn't have. Breathing a sigh of relief when I beat a rival: feeling my stomach turn over when I got beaten. These are real emotions and real motivators.

Even if you have nothing to say on the record or cannot comment on a certain issue, use any contact with a reporter as an opportunity to further the relationship and gather some information of your own. Ask what they're working on, how it's going. Offer some leads or some help. Remember, young reporters are probably lean on sources of good information and story leads. They haven't had time to build up their contact files, to gain the confidence of influential people who can help and guide them. I remember as a young reporter being so thankful for sources who, even off the record, would give me hints on where to look for stories, what experts to call, what records or databases contained the information I was seeking. If you can establish yourself as someone who can help a reporter learn the ropes, it will pay off for both sides.

Managing the media is a relationship business, first and foremost. And like any relationship, there will be good times and bad times. Whatever the case, help reporters understand why you are reacting the way you are. If there is an issue on which you can't comment, explain off the record why you can't. Offer some insight into the world of business. It will help them cover you better. If they are off-base on a story or have missed a point, tell them. Give them some direction and some other sources that will help them check it out. And pay attention to what they write. Like all of us, reporters respond to people who give them feedback on their work. They work hard and it is simple gratification. If they write a good story, compliment them. If they screw up, let them know in a non-confrontational manner. Keep the lines of communication open. By becoming a resource for them, you can develop relationships that will take you beyond the day-to-day coverage of your company. Again, goodwill can go a long way, especially if your company has a problem, which it will have some day.

## Summary of Trends

▶ *In an effort to fill space and air time, media outlets are hiring and giving greater responsibilities to inexperienced reporters.*

▶ *The talent deficit is not the reporters' fault.* The demand for them to produce has thrust them into situations in which they are in over their heads.

▶ *The competitive environment of the media is complicating the situation further.* Reporters, experienced and novice, are under increasing pressure to beat or match competitors.

▶ *These factors have created a pack mentality in business journalism similar to that seen for years in political reporting.* Without experience or expertise, reporters see safety in numbers. If everybody else is writing it or saying it, it's O.K. for them to write it or say it, too.

▶ *The conventional rules of reporting are no longer honored by many media outlets.* Checking sources and facts is now considered by many media to be less important than getting the news first. Rumor, speculation, and the fact that other outlets are reporting stories are seen as sufficient justification to publish.

▶ *There is a breakdown of command in the editorial process.* Editors and producers, the guardians of proper conduct and news judgment, are losing control of the news-gathering process.

▶ *Marketing and promotional agendas increasingly are driving the editorial agenda.* It is no longer simply enough to get the story first, you have to tell the world that you got the story first, even before it's published.

## Lessons for Companies

▶ *Understand that your role is to educate reporters about your company, because that's the only way you will get your story out properly to consumer investors.* Building a good relationship with a reporter, especially an inexperienced one, takes time and patience.

▶ *Use their inexperience as an opening to build a good relationship with young reporters, who will be thankful for your help.* It is unlikely they will always write positive things about your company, but goodwill goes a long way, no matter what the circumstances.

▶ *Remember that old war horses aren't always reliable.* They're human, too, and can get caught up in the excitement of a breaking story, even if it is based on rumor and speculation. Beware.

▶ *Don't change your strategy if faced with a media feeding frenzy.* Curb the temptation to change your response. Hold the course.

▶ *Push back, if necessary.* If you think reporters have acted irresponsibly, let them know it. The good ones will—or should—give you the courtesy of a response. If nothing else, it let's them know that you're paying attention, too. Feedback is an important part of the relationship-building process.

▶ *Pick your fights carefully.* Don't beat up on a reporter if the mistake is inadvertent and immaterial. Point out the error and if necessary request a correction. Sometimes a subtle approach is more effective, especially in a newsroom environment where the reporter may hear yelling more often than not. Again, feedback lets the reporter know that you're paying attention, and maybe he or she will be more careful next time.

▶ *Be understanding.* Reporters are people, too, under pressures and constraints. Learn what motivates them, and use this knowledge to get along better with them.

▶ *Become a resource, especially for young reporters.* Provide story leads and direction, not just information. Give them feedback, good and bad. Put some goodwill on account.

# CHAPTER 4

# Filling the Space
## The Credibility Vacuum

On the newsstand, *The New York Times* carries a story about the ongoing investigation into the murder of JonBenet Ramsay, the child beauty pageant queen who was found murdered in her Colorado home in the mid-1990s. The investigation has drifted along, without much progress, and while the little girl's parents have been the subjects of intense questioning for months, they are not official suspects. They have steadfastly declared their innocence and blamed the murder on an unknown intruder who, they say, crept into the house at night and killed their daughter. Next to the *Times* on the newsstand is *The Weekly World News*, a tabloid newspaper of *The National Enquirer* ilk. Its take on the JonBenet Ramsay investigation is that her ghost has appeared to several of the frightened investigators and told them that her parents did the deed. The story goes on to say that it is not uncommon in murder investigations for the ghosts of victims to visit an investigator, but rarely have several members of an investigative team been haunted together like this. On television, one of the tabloid news shows interviews a former reporter for one of the tabloid newspapers who was fired for not pressing hard enough to get new leads on the JonBenet Ramsay case. His dereliction of duty: He refused his editor's order to use personally damaging information about one of the investigating officers to extract information from him.

So, what's really going on in the JonBenet Ramsay case? Lots, apparently. How much of it is true? Well, at least a million readers read what *The New York Times* says. Another million or so take their news from *The Weekly World News*. And at least another million learn from television that coercion, blackmail, and payoffs are all part of the reporting game. So the question comes up again: How much of what is reported is true? How reliable are the sources you read and watch, and how reliable are the sources they use to substantiate their stories? In short, it's a question of whom you can trust. And at what point does the average American lose interest and the energy to determine which media outlet to believe? These questions are at the root of a serious credibility crisis facing the media.

## The Information Cyclotron

Tom Brokaw, "NBC Nightly News" anchor, was quoted in an article by Robert A. Crooke (*Public Relations*, 1997) as saying, "The information cycle has gotten broader, more complicated. There are more parts to it. I liken it to a kind of cyclotron in which all sorts of information and information sources are blended together and delivered in the same channels. But they are not all at the same level of truth or accuracy."

For the media, the need to get the news first, make it look good, and get it right at the same time is an elusive task. They will either spend more money to do it, or they will simply change the rules of what constitutes responsible journalism. The latter is a much cheaper way to go. It would be nice to think that at some point there will be so much media—perhaps we're at that point already—there will be a fallout: fewer players, but ideally with a higher aggregate quality. Instead, the trend seems to be going in the opposite direction. There are more news shows, or quasi-news shows, every day. It seems anyone who looks good on camera can become involved in some sort of journalism, whether qualified or not.

Your company can get trapped in this situation. With so many media outlets, there is a great temptation to be everywhere. But a company that spreads itself too thin risks diluting its message and damaging its reputation. It will get caught in Tom Brokaw's "information cyclotron," in which the good information becomes indistinguishable from the bad.

Of course, what's so easily forgotten is that audiences will suffer the most. They will continue to lose trust in the messages they receive and the media through which they receive them. This comes at a time when these audiences—particularly the consumer-investor audience—are seeking better information and insight from better media sources. They want to believe that the information they receive is reliable and that any accompanying opinion and analysis are trustworthy as well.

Faced with this problem, the media in general and the business media in particular would do well to learn a lesson from advertising. For some time, there has been a definable decrease in the average consumer's trust in advertising and a marked decrease in the real and perceived power of advertising. Bert Manning, retired chairman and chief executive of J. Walter Thompson Worldwide, a global advertising agency, addressed the American Association of Advertising Agencies' 1996 annual meeting on negative political advertising. "We have this huge credibility gap, and I know it is from political advertising," he said. In particular, he blamed the "smear and scare" approach of political ads for the massive consumer distrust in all advertising.

It would follow that the decline of advertising credibility has raised the power of the editorial word. If people don't trust advertising anymore, the next best thing is the news, printed or otherwise. Indeed, the business media have a huge opportunity to capitalize on the trend. The Siskel and Ebertizing of America—the demand of consumers to have a third-party endorsement of a product or service to help them make decisions—is presumably a phenomenon ready-made for increased editorial credibility. But the media have dropped the ball. And so have many of the companies who should be holding themselves and the media with whom they work to higher standards for the sake of their customers.

## Distrust of the Media

Here is an example of how the credibility vacuum is only partially the media's fault: I worked with a client for many years who managed a big core business for a major financial institution. He was truly a guru of the business and widely recognized by his peers as such. His knowledge of the business and the people in it was so valuable that he was constantly sought after by the media to discuss issues and trends and give guidance on all sorts of matters. There was only one problem: He refused to speak to the media, and here's why: He believed the media made everything up, that every word in every newspaper and on television was a fabrication.

I was startled by his naïveté. After all, he had been in the business for a long time and knew the way the world worked. He was no greenhorn. And he was not just kidding about the media. There was no malice or bravado in his stance. In fact, as a soft-spoken fellow whose first love was financial statements, he was not the kind of person who joked a lot. He simply believed it did not matter what he or anyone else told a reporter; the reporter would make up the story according to how he or she wanted the story to appear.

His distrust of the media came to light during an exchange with a trade publication reporter who was seeking guidance on a story. The reporter didn't want any on-the-record comments; she only wanted to discuss with him a theory she was pursuing. He refused to speak with her and told me, "She's wrong, but no matter what I tell her, she'll make it up anyway."

Having spent a good part of my career in journalism and several years at so-called prestigious publications, I was fascinated by this belief that media outlets make stuff up. Maybe I was the one who was being naïve, having always striven to be as responsible as possible. I was aware of the periodic reports of journalists who fabricated stories and were caught. These included the sensational story of the defrocking of a *Washington Post* reporter who won a Pulitzer Prize in the 1980s for a story about an inner-city cocaine baby who did not exist. Like any profession, I believed that journalism had its share of bad apples, but they were far from the norm. So I was intrigued to see whether this attitude about the media was isolated to a few nonbelievers or whether it had a broader following.

During research for this book, I was disappointed to learn that the average person's trust of the media is very low. This distrust is rooted in the public's lack of confidence that the media can get a story right as well as in a strong belief that the media makes up facts to enhance the entertainment value of a story. People not only believe this happens, they expect it to happen. And they adjust their expectations accordingly.

Furthermore, many people believe that all media, even the so-called responsible media, pay their contacts for stories. Many people assume that a person whose name and face appear in the press receives some sort of compensation. Still others believe that reporters will do absolutely anything, including extortion, blackmail, and threats, to extract information from people. To hear the tabloid reporter who lost his job tell it, his editor was adamant about exposing an undisclosed personal problem of the JonBenet Ramsay investigator—a problem unrelated in any way to the case—as a way to pressure the police officer to cooperate. Why the reporter, who had been with the paper for some time, decided at that point to have a surge of conscience and journalistic integrity was unclear. But his story offered a compelling glimpse of the dark side of journalism.

Where do companies fit into this equation? It is easy to sit back and criticize the media for publishing or broadcasting trash because they have space and time to fill. But in business news, it is up to companies to step forward and fill the vacuum with useful information. The opportunity is there. In a world hungrier for steak than sizzle, companies can begin to close the media credibility vacuum. There is danger in not doing it or not doing it properly. Here's an example:

# TWA Flight 800: A Credibility Crisis

When TWA Flight 800 exploded and crashed into the Atlantic Ocean off Long Island, New York, in 1997, rumors about the cause of the crash outnumbered the fragments of wreckage pulled from the water: a terrorist bomb, aviation fuel fumes over-heated by air-conditioning machinery that ignited shortly after takeoff, a missile launched from a ship as part of a vast covert operation that required thousands of military and government personnel at all levels to keep their mouths shut. There was even an eyewitness, interviewed ad nauseum by television crews, who claimed to have seen the fiery tail of the missile rocket appear out of the night sky and connect with the plane as it climbed toward its cruising altitude, bound for Europe.

Bomb, mechanical failure, missile. The media chased all the rumors, and many reported them as fact before there was any evidence. Television programs showed elaborate graphics that gave eerie credence to even the most preposterous theories. It's no wonder that many viewers were convinced of the authentic-ity of the theory. Why would someone go to such great lengths to create a fancy graphic if there weren't even a grain of truth to it? The media were on a roller coaster of proposed theory-denial-new proposed theory. The question of what happened was answered differently almost hourly, depending on which news-cast you had seen last. In the early days following the crash, care-ful, conventional media outlets such as *The New York Times* were criticized for lagging behind the story—the *Times* reported only the facts it could confirm, leaving it near the back of the pack in the rumor-du-jour sweepstakes. Tired investigators spent much of their daily press conferences addressing rumor, not fact, and dismissing news stories that had already appeared as fact.

Then came Pierre Salinger. Until his foray into the morass of TWA Flight 800, this venerable news guru and former press secre-tary to the late U.S. Attorney General Robert Kennedy, was a respected journalist. He entered the stalled investigation into the cause of the crash as the proponent of the missile theory. He claimed to have evidence that proved such an attack. It was later discounted.

The confluence of events surrounding and following the crash of Flight 800 provides an important lesson on how quickly situations can get out of hand if those involved are not prepared for the unexpected, and how empty media space can be filled with speculation, much of it incorrect. The resulting credibility vacuum is an issue that the media must face and correct. And the companies covered by the media must take some responsibility, too, to ensure that the space is filled with fact and informed opinion, not speculation.

With the TWA crash, the credibility vacuum appeared within minutes of the explosion. As reports of the crash spread, some families and friends of the victims assembled. But no authority at the airport could give them any information. For TWA, this was a critical point in the event. No one expected the gate agents or ticket takers or any other crew members to have solid information about what had happened less than an hour earlier more than a hundred miles away over open ocean. But the head of the company should have recognized that something had gone terribly wrong. Within the next few hours, the airport would be flooded with people, including the media, seeking information. The airline needed someone there immediately to take charge of the situation.

Of primary concern should have been the families and friends of the victims. More than anyone else, they, had a close, personal interest in the safety of the flight. They had the most to lose. And as crisis public relations experts know, in situations like this, the handling of victims and their families is paramount to managing the entire event. The reason: The emotional involvement is so high and the possibility of shock so great that they become liabilities to themselves and the truth. When told that loved ones have died, no matter what the circumstances, these people will get upset, they will get angry, and they will want answers. But first, they will want a place to sit down, someone to talk to, someone who can assure them that everything is being done to bring them information and answers, someone to be sympathetic to their grief.

The early arrivals at JFK that evening got none of that. For hours, they milled around, getting more upset and angrier by the minute. Tidbits of information would arrive along with other concerned parties who had heard snippets of the story on the news. And then the media began to arrive—crews, cameras, recorders, and notebooks. They were looking for two things: a spokesperson for the airline to give them some information and the all-important reaction shots of the crowd.

The media found lots of reaction shots but not much airline response. In fact, much of the reaction from the crowd was anger at the airline for not being more responsive, for not having set up a system for dispensing information. By the time senior spokespeople for the airline arrived to set up a conference in the middle of the night, many of the families had left to find places to spend the night. When the families and friends returned the next morning, they were faced with the same void. At that point, TWA had two crises on its hands—an airliner was down somewhere over the Atlantic under unexplained circumstances, and an angry mob was telling the world through television, radio, and print that it was receiving no assistance whatsoever. Worse, consumers of the media really had no idea what was going on, except that a plane had crashed and there were a lot of very unhappy people in New York.

Of little concern to the loved ones of the victims but probably not lost on the executives of the airline was the fact that the crash came at a crucial time for TWA. Dogged for years by financial and performance problems, the airline was on the verge of launching a huge new image and equipment update program. A crash, while an occupational hazard in the airline industry, was a major blow to the effort. The airline's inability to manage its aftermath properly added salt to the wound.

The credibility gap widened as the investigation moved forward. The relatives of the dead were so angry with TWA that once the airline began to give them information, they received it with a great deal of skepticism. Compounding the problem was the fact that the crash had occurred over water. The wreckage lay at the bottom of the ocean, making the recovery effort slow and dangerous for search crews. Bad weather and swirling tides made finding and raising wreckage a painstaking task. With each day that passed, as silt-covered debris and currents moved lighter objects away, the possibility of finding all the clues in the mystery became less likely. Still, the mammoth effort continued, the wreckage was slowly recovered, and the plane was reassembled in a hangar on Long Island not far from the crash site. The Federal Bureau of Investigation and the National Transportation Safety Board (NTSB) jointly participated in the investigation, examining millions of pieces of evidence and interviewing thousands of people directly and indirectly involved with the crash. They even staged simulations with other 747 aircraft to test theories. In the end, the investigators concluded that a mechanical glitch, perhaps complicated by a design flaw, had caused the explosion that brought down the airliner. From what they could determine, the crash was an accident.

Throughout this painful disaster, it was very difficult for the average viewer, listener, or reader to determine what was a credible report. So damaging was the media coverage of TWA 800 that when John F. Kennedy Jr.'s plane crashed off Martha's Vineyard in 1999, NTSB officials pleaded with the media no to report speculation. It is an important lesson on the quest for credibility that the news media are losing. The premium on pretty faces, the insatiable demand for content to fill acres of newsprint and hours of air time, and the dearth of experienced talent have created a credibility vacuum in business news. It presents a serious problem for the news media, the companies that communicate through them, and the audiences that rely on them for information.

## How to Use the Media

What can your company do to offset the dangers of this media environment? You must first understand the reporting process. Don't be like my former client, who believed that all reporters are frauds. They aren't, particularly in the business media. They don't make stuff up. They don't pay sources for information. Some may be inexperienced and a little fast and loose with facts, but few are malicious. Most are too afraid of getting in trouble and losing their jobs. Learn who the reporters are and how they do their jobs. Ask around. Find out who's good and who isn't. Gathering this kind of intelligence is really no different from what you do in your business.

Then, rely on your own standards to decide which media sources you can trust. If you're like most Americans, you rely on a variety of sources for your daily dose of information. Just by habit, you choose outlets for hard news, business news, weather, sports, and entertainment. You may use only one or two, or you may use several. Common sense can go a long way in helping you understand the media. If you need more evidence, talk to your friends and colleagues. Ask your customers, too. You can learn a lot about people's tastes by talking to them about their media preferences. Consider it a different form of market research. Find out where they get their information, what sources they trust. Whose opinions do they seek in the media when it comes to making important decisions?

As a media consultant, the first thing I ask clients who have or want to become involved in dealing with the media is what media they like and don't like. I want to know which outlets they consider to be credible and which they consider to be lacking. I also like to know what causes them to have these opinions. Most are surprised at how many different outlets they use in a day and how specialized their tastes are. One client claimed that he never had time to pay much attention to the news. But when we sat down and documented his daily intake of media, it was pretty substantial—he woke up to the news on his clock radio, half-watched, half-listened to a morning news show on television while he dressed, read at least the front pages of every section in the daily paper while he ate breakfast, listened to the radio on his drive to the office, sometimes went online to check out a news site such as CNN.com or a financial site, and usually watched a bit of the late night news before he went to bed. So while he did not spend long stretches of time with any one media outlet, in the aggregate, he probably spent an average of ninety minutes a day watching, listening, and reading the news. He was surprised not only at the number of media outlets he used, but also at how almost unconsciously he had become adept at choosing specific media for his specific needs. In effect, he was customizing his media intake without even thinking about it.

One of the most fascinating curiosities of media tastes appears every day in New York City. In the morning, the subways and commuter trains are full of people reading *The Wall Street Journal* and *The New York Times*. On the ride home, however, these same people are more likely to be reading *The New York Daily News* or *The New York Post*. In fact, the biggest crossover readership—a newspaper term that helps newspapers track the competitive tastes of its customers—is from *The New York Times* to the *Daily News* or the *Post*. Strange bedfellows? Not really. Ask the readers, and they will tell you that for credible world, national, and business news, they choose the *Times*. For in-depth business reporting, the paper of record is *The Wall Street Journal*. But after a long day at work, there's nothing like a little light entertainment and humor from tabloids. And besides, many say the sports coverage in the tabs, including Long Island's *Newsday*, is superb.

By understanding a little more about how and why you use the media, you can start to understand how your company can pick its spots when seeking to fill the credibility vacuum. You will get a very good idea about which media you prefer to carry your messages and which you don't. Of course, sometimes you don't have a choice. But managing the media is not an exact science. You will get zinged. You will run across a reporter who's a bad apple once in a while. Still, if you can put together a relatively clear picture of the media universe in which you and your peers operate, you will be ahead of the game.

## Summary of Trends

> ▶ *The drive by the media to get it first, rather than get it right, has created a credibility vacuum for the media and for consumers who read, watch, and listen.*

▶ *The reporting of speculation has become standard procedure: Report the rumor first, get the facts later.*

▶ *Shotgun journalism is in style.* If a reporter can get someone to respond to a question, no matter how ridiculous it is, that is enough to constitute a story. A story that is denied—even if the denial is backed up with fact—does not simply die. The denial becomes a story in itself.

▶ *The lowering of standards by some media has tarnished the reputation of responsible media outlets.* Their dilemma is whether to lower their own standards to be competitive.

▶ *Viewers and readers are increasingly confused and distrustful of the media.* It is now more difficult to separate fact from fiction. More people think the media "just make it up," pay their sources, or coerce them into talking. Again, this has had the most impact on the so-called responsible press because consumers are finding it more difficult to distinguish between reliable media reports and unreliable ones.

▶ *The media are heading for a fall, at least among the more sophisticated consumer-investors.* The level of trust will decline to the point where, like advertising, few will believe in the validity of the media's messages.

## Lessons for Companies:

▶ *Companies must be aggressive in taking their share of responsibility for filling the credibility vacuum.*

▶ *Blaming the media environment does not help.* You must find ways to get credible messages about your company to the audiences who matter most.

► *If you think a media outlet is suspect, the increasingly sophisticated consumer-investor thinks so, too.* Determine which media outlets you consider to be credible and develop relationships with them. Avoid those you consider to be liabilities.

► *In a crisis, a credibility vacuum can make the situation worse.* Speculation, fueled by emotion, is a dangerous mix. Be prepared. Be responsive.

# CHAPTER 5

# Gen-X Journalism
## The Mouse That Roared

S teven S. Ross says in the 1998 Middleberg/Ross Media in Cyberspace Study that with online services "many readers can be on the scene first. We, as journalists, should continue to try to report quickly, of course, but we can only compete in the long run by telling the story in a more understandable way and in a more complete way. The tools are in place. The brain power is there, too, but in limited quantities. We need more journalists capable of handling complex issues, of diving for detail and explaining implications. The question is not whether we'll have the programming to fill the bandwidth, but whether we'll have the brain power on the beat."

In late 1998, after months of relative quiet, PaineWebber once again found itself in the takeover rumor mill. Speculation had been heavy among journalists and industry observers about the firm's possible link-ups with any number of competitors, banks, and insurance companies. So, to be back on the radar screen was nothing new. But this time, the way the rumors spread and the speed with which they turned into news were new.

I learned about the rumor at 3 A.M. one Tuesday when my telephone rang at home, startling me from a sound sleep. It was a reporter from Bloomberg in London, who had picked up chatter on the Internet that Dresdner Bank, one of the largest and best-

known German institutions, had expressed interest in PaineWebber. It was news to me, I told him, and served up the usual policy
comment that it was the firm's policy not to discuss speculation
about the firm for the record. I left a voicemail for my boss at the
office, alerting her to the inquiry, and went back to bed. An hour
later, the phone rang again. This time, it was a reporter from
Frankfurt, Germany, who had heard the same rumor in an online
chat room. Reuters New York called next, saying the chat rooms
and e-mails were on fire about a possible PaineWebber-Dresdner
link.

By the time I reached the office, the morning television and
radio outlets were reporting the story, and my voicemail was full
of messages from reporters seeking comment. Online, articles
had already started to appear on the business news services, my
e-mail was overloaded, and the various chat rooms were full of
exchanges about the possibility of a merger. Many online writers
were already weighing the pros and cons of such a partnership
and crunching numbers. The number of hits had almost tripled
on the PaineWebber's Web site, where the firm posts all sorts of
company information, including financial news releases and
annual reports. In a matter of minutes, reporters had gathered
enough information to flesh out what was essentially a one-fact—
or one-rumor—story. The consequences of this wild rush of
"news" stories were serious for PaineWebber. The stock fluctu-
ated, because of a very real expectation among investors—based
on false information—that the firm could not fulfill.

The fact that the rumor was unsubstantiated is beside the
point. What matters is that the online world has become not only
a breeding ground for news and the transfer of information but
also a growing source for story ideas and substantiating facts for
journalists of all stripes.

## The Online Phenomenon

The transformation of business journalism has been created by the
way the new generation of reporters approaches its work. The

demographics experts call this group Generation X, people in their late 20's and 30's. But it really applied to anyone with a reliance on and comfort with technology. Reporters at most news organizations have data bases at their disposal and can cruise the Internet effortlessly. The result is a smaller world in which news travels faster and more efficiently from companies to consumers and back. Like the reporters who report the stories, readers today are as likely to call up news on their personal computers or Bloomberg terminals as they are to read it in the newspaper or watch it on television.

In effect, technology and these new journalists' familiarity with it has made them instant experts. Unlike in the old days, when reporters slogged through paper clippings in newspaper morgues, most newsroom computers now give users instant access to a wide array of data bases. Even someone filling in for a regular beat reporter can, in a very short time, gather enough information to establish an angle and ask tough questions. The biggest mistake a company can make is being unprepared.

For example, public companies should know that every regulatory filing they make is immediately available on Edgar, the Securities and Exchange Commission's electronic database. Reporters can go online at any time and get the information. It is not uncommon, in fact, for information to appear on Edgar before it has been disseminated throughout the company. If it is a material disclosure and something that is likely to generate media coverage, companies should be aware of this. You do not want to find yourself in a situation where the reporter has more complete information than the spokespeople for your company. If they don't have access to the Internet and Edgar, they should get it. It's one thing to be surprised. It's another to be embarrassed by an outsider who knows more about what's going on in your company than you do.

## The Media in Cyberspace Study

To fully understand the online phenomenon, you should read the annual Media in Cyberspace Study published jointly by Steven Ross,

associate professor at the Columbia University Graduate School of
Journalism in New York, and Don Middleberg, chief executive of Middleberg + Associates, a New York public relations firm that specializes
in online communications. The 1999 study, the fifth of its kind, was
sent to 3,400 newspaper and magazine editors throughout the
United States, including all daily newspapers and Sunday-only
papers.

The study has quickly become the gospel for companies and
public relations executives who want to understand the sweeping
changes that are affecting the dynamics of reporting as well as the
relationships companies and their public relations counselors have
with members of the media. It is also useful for the media, in that
the growing pains they are experiencing as they try to manage the
power and influence of this new communications channel
threaten to damage their already weakened credibility.

For those of you who still consider the Internet and online
communications a fad or think they have a limited influence on
your life and business, the findings may startle you. Among them:

> *Almost all journalists now use online tools for researching
> and reporting.* Most use them for gathering images
> and other materials that had to be physically delivered
> to the newsroom just a few years ago. More than half
> use them for distributing news as well. Publications are
> distributing their print versions online, and many are
> beginning to publish original content online. In addi-
> tion, joint newsrooms, shared by print and Web oper-
> ations, are on the rise.

> *While most journalists prefer live sources for breaking
> news, they will turn to the Web if they can't make con-
> tact.* With the evolution of the 24-hour news cycle, we
> expect this trend to continue.

> *Newspapers, which tended to keep their newsrooms sep-
> arate at the start of the new media age in 1994, have*

*now joined their print and new media sides.* Operations are completely shared in more than half of the nation's Web newsrooms. They are totally separate in only 13 percent. In fact, newspapers and magazines are now quite similar in their accommodations for new media.

▶ *For handling new sources or new providers of story ideas, magazine journalists rank the telephone first (42 percent), followed by e-mail (26 percent), and in-person contact (19 percent).* Newspaper journalists want to see whom they are dealing with; in-person contact is a strong first choice (56 percent), with e-mail (16 percent) and phone (20 percent) far behind.

▶ *Original content on Web sites grew enormously in 1998.* Most heartening, growth was at the low end of the scale. In 1997, 39 percent of the newspaper respondents with Web sites said the sites had less than 5 percent original content. In 1999 only 22 percent of the newspaper respondents reported original content on Web sites—a huge cut in one year! For magazines, the drop was from 27 percent to 11 percent—nearly threefold. Thus, 1998 marks a historic moment: News organizations have now clearly broken away from their tendency to use online technology (Web sites usually, but not always) as a distribution device more than as a new medium.

▶ *Growth in Internet access among journalists has increased enormously in the past few years and now approaches universality.* Only 2 percent of respondents to this year's survey either said they had no access or did not answer the question at all. Contrast that figure with 37 percent of the comparable sample in the fall 1995 survey and 9 percent last year.

Almost six out of every 10 respondents to this question say their publication, or portions of it, are already online. That's a small increase from 1997 and double the 25 percent recorded in 1995. Only 6 percent of the magazine respondents said they have no plans to go online. Only 10 percent of the newspaper respondents said they have no plans.

▶ *More than a third of the publications with Web sites allow the Web to scoop their print product, at least sometimes.* That's up slightly from 1997.

▶ *About 41 percent of the sample (compared to an almost identical 40 percent last year and 42 percent in 1996) writes copy that ends up on their own publication's online service (Web site, usually).* Another 6 percent freelance for other organizations' sites (the same as the past two years). But only a handful (1 percent of the sample) write exclusively for online services (also the same as the past two years).

▶ *Overall, almost half (48 percent) of the respondents now say they or their staff go online every day.* Another 32 percent go online at least weekly.

▶ *Razzle-dazzle doesn't sway journalists.* This suggests that opening a site with a fast-loading home page, then providing a "journalist's track," is still a good strategy if the site is to serve as an entryway for the press to get data.

▶ *Use of the Web for press releases and for reading online has grown substantially.* Use for getting images is up a bit. The overall pattern suggests that non-Web Internet uses have been getting short shrift from today's journalists.

▶ *Journalists use of the Web is gaining in breaking news sit-uations.* After hours or in a crisis, journalists for both magazines and newspapers are most likely to call "other interested parties/community groups/emer-gency services" first. Magazine journalists are most likely to call industry experts next and go to the com-pany's Web site third. Newspaper journalists say they'd go to the Web next and call industry experts third.

▶ *Photos and camera-ready art, along with electronic images, are strongly preferred over slides and other trans-parency forms; slides are preferred by only about one edi-tor in ten.*

▶ *Businesses still have a Web-site credibility gap compared to nonprofit organizations.* Journalists do use business sites, however.

▶ *Journalists still get their story ideas the old-fashioned way—from sources, story leads provided in person, and press releases.* But story ideas from the Web are increas-ingly used.

## The Implication for Business

The implications of these trends is enormous for companies from a public relations standpoint. According to Middleberg:

> The impact of the information age continues to have far reaching dramatic effects on the public relations industry and the interaction between the media and communications practitioners. The increasing influx of new content, new public forums, the launch of new publications and the con-tinuous advance of developing technologies have resulted in new outlets, new messages, new audi-

ences, and, most significantly, new ways to communicate.

Although there will never be a substitute for
face-to-face communications with journalists, the
new media are revolutionizing public relations
techniques as we know them. As real-time news
cycles and online scoops continue to shake the
historic operations of print and broadcast media,
the PR professional must adjust accordingly. In
addition, the promise of widespread broadband
delivery allows for the presentation of more elaborate messages in a richer interactive format—
new tools driving new ways to tell new stories.

Public relations practitioners not truly incorporating Internet communications initiatives into
their public relations strategies are doing a disser-
vice to their clients and to the media. To dismiss
this new generation of media in cyberspace and
the online communications they prefer is incom-
petent and borders on negligence.

The ascent of online communities and
forums is providing unique opportunities to
deliver one-on-one messages to consumers.
Increasingly, PR practitioners are able to target
their audiences directly and circumvent editors
and journalists, and some would argue that the
most successful public relations practitioners
today have learned to use the new media to 'tran-
scend the translators.' This development requires
the expansion of the public relations professional's
role and skills into new areas, demanding new
marketing, consulting and technical abilities.

While building relationships with the media
remains the core value of public relations, PR pro-

fessionals need to take a hard look at the Internet and ways to deliver messages directly to the consumer's desktop. Firms that develop their knowledge base to tackle the demands of new communications will certainly lead the industry.

The implications of journalists' extensive use of the Internet are huge for PR firms and how they can best help businesses deal with media.

▶ *While the online world wields mass-media power similar to that of traditional broadcast and print media, the Internet will not serve as a substitute for personal contact.* The Internet's greatest power lies in its use as a communications tool to supplement and enhance traditional communications objectives.

▶ *With the amount of original content on the Internet increasing every year, PR practitioners have new outlets to pitch and new ways to pitch them.* Journalists writing for print publications may have time and space limitations, but with the potentially limitless publishing space of the Internet and its ability to capitalize on the twenty-four-hour news cycle, online journalists often have fewer deadline constraints and room for extra copy.

▶ *Increased bandwidth, interactivity, and multimedia mean that communicators need to learn to tell stories in nonlinear ways.* Multimedia storytelling may become the PR practitioner's most valuable online skill.

▶ *Journalists are visiting corporate Web sites to get press releases, important news, and financial information.* They are also going to the Web during major news events or crisis situations. This suggests that the media expect leading companies and trade associations to provide comprehensive and accurate information on their Web sites. Up-to-date and easily searchable information in online press rooms is becoming the norm.

▶ *Journalists are using more e-mail for communications with sources, once preliminary contact has been established.* To avoid eroding relationships with journalists and endangering e-mail effectiveness, PR professionals must avoid "spam" at all costs. The media are being bogged down by junk e-mail, blast press releases, and irrelevant messages, and have responded in the past year by reducing the attention they pay to such e-mail. Establishing relationships with journalists is just as important online.

▶ *With many journalists turning first to search engines and directories like Yahoo! and Alta Vista to locate information, it is more important than ever for organizations to be listed prominently in the major search engines.* Advanced PR practitioners need to understand how journalists find information online to ensure their information is easy to find.

▶ *The speed with which information travels on the Internet, whether accurate or not, is of great concern.* Inaccurate or outdated information, rumors, or mistaken fact can quickly spread, damaging brand identity and reputation. Online monitoring and being prepared to respond to cyber crises will play a bigger role in the future for public relations practitioners.

▶ *More and more stories are breaking online as news organizations are scooping their own print outlets by publishing first online.* With increased competition in the media business, we expect this trend to continue. As a result, the traditional media are following the online media and expanding upon stories that originate on the Internet. Working with the online media is just as important as working with print and broadcast media.

▶ *Journalists want Web sites to be organized to answer fol-low-up questions rather than initial queries.* But company Web sites have to field "initial queries" from the general public as well. Thus, "crisis communications" sites must have a split personality. Either there must be a clear "journalist" track, or journalists need a separate site or separate section of the site that is not necessarily openly linked to the site home page.

# A Question of Brain Power

The downside of the media's cyber excitement is, as Ross noted in the study, that the technology has advanced far beyond the capabilities of the people using it. There is a very real danger that there isn't enough brain power among journalists to handle this new world. Think of a Ferrari sports car in the hands of an inexperienced driver. Think of an automatic weapon in the hands of a child. Think of any situation in which the machinery being used is far more advanced than the person operating it, and you've got the idea.

And if you think it's a only a minor problem, think again. A former colleague of mine from *The New York Times* was recruited recently by one of the top online news services in New York to be an editor for its business news section. After many years at the *Times,* the change would be refreshing, he thought. But after only a few weeks, he called me in a panic. The place was full of inexperienced reporters who knew very little about business yet were under immense pressure to find and write dirt about publicly traded companies. Many did not like to have their copy edited, a sure sign of inexperience, as any senior reporter at *The New York Times* or *The Wall Street Journal* will tell you. Some refused to answer questions from editors. Others would not return telephone calls or e-mails from editors seeking clarification on a point or answers to questions. Some reporters, he said, would even complain to the newsroom's managers that they were unhappy their work was being edited at all.

The dangers represented by this lack of checks and balances, which is crucial when dealing with complicated information, were obvious. Editors were under so much pressure to move copy that the usual process of confirming information and having reporters answer questions about facts in the story was often sidestepped. I was also startled to learn that the whole operation works on a computer system that is programmed to allow only a set amount of time for the reporter and editor to work on a story. When the time is up, the story is automatically posted to the Web. In effect, stories are posted online whether the information is confirmed or not. It is not uncommon, he told me, for incomplete stories to be posted full of errors and omissions.

A system like this scares an editor who has been trained by *The New York Times* with its careful rules about accuracy and fairness. It scared my colleague enough to make him realize he was wrong for online journalism. The fact that this fast and loose style of journalism was used in the coverage of publicly traded companies was a serious liability to him and anyone who wrote or handled copy. He was worried that eventually the system would bite him. He could be in a lawsuit born of a story that was poorly reported, filled with incorrect or incomplete information, and published live on the Internet before it could be corrected, thanks to the efficiency of technology. Without much hesitation, he quit after only a short time. Yet the service continues to operate, generating billions of bytes of information, right and wrong, about companies large and small.

## Incorporating Online Communication

So as the manager of a company, what can you do to begin to manage this process? The first thing is to get help from people who know not only about online technology but also about public relations and media relations. They are hard to find. There is a bit of a talent deficit on that side of the computer terminal as well. It's not hard to find people who are very skilled at the technology: There is a whole generation out there who cruises the Internet effortlessly, many of whom can design, build, and program Web sites. There are also a lot of good public relations professionals who know not only how to handle the media, but also how to help a company develop a communications strategy, hammer out key messages, and train company spokespeople to deliver those messages effectively. The problem is, there are very few people who can do both. Recruiters across the country are scrambling to find qualified candidates as the demand for these types of professionals skyrockets at companies and public relations agencies alike. In time, perhaps, as online communications and the demand for a combination of skills grow, a new breed of online communications specialists will crop up. Many public relations agencies, in fact, are trying to create greenhouses in which these people can develop. At Middleberg + Associates in New York, for example, people get training in the fundamentals of public relations and the newest technology.

Another step your company can take is to hire an online monitoring service. These services use various methods to track any number of online sites, including chat rooms, bulletin boards, Webzines, and news services, to determine what is being said about their company clients. They also can look for rogue Web sites or the misuse of your company's name or logo, which are legal issues more than public relations issues. We'll talk more about monitoring in the next chapter.

It is also a good idea to take some of the pointers from the Middleberg/Ross study and update your company's Web site, if you have one: And if you don't, you need to create one immediately. You can't afford not to have one. If, as the study suggests, the media will use business Web sites more and more as sources of information and as an interactive gateway for dialogue with companies, it is worth your while to have a site that can accommodate that need. And remember, forget the razzle-dazzle when it comes to the media section of the site. If you use a designer, do not let him or her talk you into fancy graphics or pretty pictures. The media part of a side should be simple, straightforward, and easy to use. Function, not form, should be the watchword.

Many companies have resisted the temptation to experiment with online newsrooms and interactive chat functions mainly because they have not had qualified people to monitor the site. If you don't have this capability on your site, build it. And if you don't have someone who knows how to work in that environment comfortably, hire someone. It will probably be one of the most important investments you make. But the most important thing you can do is to get yourself and the senior management of your company familiar with what's going on online. If there is someone within the company who can give you an introductory course on the basics, have that person start immediately. If you don't, hire someone. Most public relations agencies with Internet operations have people who train executives in this field.

Of course, you'll benefit by learning how to use the new technology. But you'll also gain a new image for yourself as the with-it, tech-savvy executive. There is an important perceptual advantage as well. For example, I was working with a client who was the chief executive officer of a company in the financial services industry, which was undergoing sweeping change, mainly because of technology. Technology was changing the way customers received and managed information. It was also changing the relationship the customers had with the companies in the business. The customers were demanding more and better technology for everything from account management to transacting business to exchanging information, analysis, and strategic ideas with their account representatives. It was important, therefore, for the company not only to have the technological capability to meet these needs, but to be perceived as a technologically savvy company. To be seen as ahead of the curve in terms of technology was considered by senior management to be a competitive advantage, and every company in the industry was trying to portray itself as a leader in this area.

## Making the Effort

Enter the media. Some reporters wanted to see whether the claims about online savvy were real or just a smokescreen. A young reporter who covered online technology for *The Wall Street Journal* decided to flush out the impostors. She wanted to write an article that looked not at what the companies were doing about technology but at the technology habits of the senior executives who ran them. Armed with a list of half a dozen questions, she polled the chief executives' offices of several big companies. She wanted very basic information: Do you use the Internet? For what purposes? How much time do you spend online each day or each week? Do you have any favorite sites?

My client was concerned. He hardly ever spent any time online. The computer was on a lot at home where his children cruised the Web and he and his wife periodically used the Internet to check out movie schedules. But he did not spend time at home or at the office searching the Web for information or using it to communicate. Like his mail and other correspondence that came to his office, his e-mail was sorted and answered by assistants. At the same time, the company had made a big push to position itself as a technology-smart entity. It had invested a lot of time and money in telling the world that it was online and that it knew what it was doing. The contrast, my client feared, between the company's message and his own personal lack of online proficiency would be embarrassing.

To handle the situation, we recommended he do the interview because we believed it was an important part of building the company's image to have the chief executive included in an article about technology. Besides, the company's public stance on technology basically committed it to participate. My client feared the company would have been conspicuous in its absence.

But we also made sure to brief the reporter that, as a chief executive of a big company, our client didn't spend a lot of time cruising the Web during the workday because he didn't have that much spare time to spend. By the same token, he didn't watch a

lot of television or chat on the telephone at work. Chief executives rarely have that luxury. The same was true for his time away
from the office. Spending hours online or in front of the tube just
wasn't possible. The reporter appreciated his candor and took the
point. But she was still interested in learning what he *did* know
about the Internet. With a little coaching, he showed a limited
but growing knowledge of the online universe, and the reporter
was most appreciative of his participation. We agreed that as he
was bound to participate, he did a good job.

For days after the interview, we waited for the article to
appear. I would call the reporter periodically to see when we
might expect it. Now, of course, for competitive reasons, reporters
usually won't give away a publication date or the exact angle of
the stories on which they are working. And while this reporter was
usually forthcoming, she was a little more reticent than usual
about this story. That struck me as odd. This was not an earth-shat-
tering, news-breaking story on which the fortunes of companies
could rise and fall. This was a light feature that might give a few
people a chuckle over their coffee in the morning.

Finally, months later, when the article still had not appeared, I
called the reporter one more time. She confided in me that the story
didn't run because she could only get a couple of the chief executives
to talk to her—my client and maybe one other. It was funny, she said,
how these executives were always anxious to talk to her about business issues, but when asked about their personal expertise on the Internet, they hid. "I guess they were scared," I suggested. She agreed.

So in the end, the participation of my client was valuable, but
not in the way we had expected when we agreed to the interview.
First, we won credibility with the reporter, not a small feat when
you consider that she is on the hottest beat with the most influential business news organization in the country. Second, we successfully completed a dry run for our client and alerted him to the
fact that the online issue was generating more and more attention
and would continue to do so. He could expect more inquiries like
this one. So it would be worth his while to learn a little more about
what was going on in cyberspace. Because, as I told him, you can

bet your competitors who didn't return the reporter's call are taking crash courses on the Internet right now. They'll be ready the next time a reporter calls. And you should be, too.

# Summary of Trends

▶ *Reporters are almost universally including online technology as a news-gathering tool.* As the systems become more advanced and reporters become more comfortable with the technology, cyber journalism will grow.

▶ *Online technology has changed the dynamics of journalism.* Not only is news gathering and publishing a twenty-four-hour-a-day, seven-day-a-week process, but information moves around the world in seconds as well.

▶ *There is a subculture of opinion lurking in cyberspace in the form of chat rooms, bulletin boards, and personal sites.* Discussions about your company can take place online without your knowing about them.

▶ *Like other parts of the media, online journalism is experiencing growing pains.* There is a talent deficit. Online news services are populated with inexperienced reporters who are not skilled at reporting on publicly traded companies.

▶ *Online technology is more advanced than the people using it.* Like a sports car in the hands of an inexperienced driver, online journalism is being driven fast by a human element that is not skilled enough to control it. The danger of crashes is very real.

▶ *On the public relations side, there is a talent deficit, too.* Finding executives who are skilled in both the technical side and the media relations side is difficult. Demand for these people will continue to grow.

▶ *Public relations professionals and agencies that do not incorporate online communications into their mix will hurt the image of the clients they represent.* A company that is perceived to be lagging behind the technology curve will lose goodwill and open itself up for criticism.

# Lessons for Companies

▶ *Meet the demands of the online media by making sure the company's Web sites are useful tools that reporters can rely on for information and access.* This should be a top priority.

▶ *Hire at least one person to be responsible for online communications and maintaining the media relations segment of the corporate Web site.* Ideally, this person should have the technical skills necessary to feel comfortable online and a fundamental understanding of media relations issues.

▶ *Hire a monitoring service to see what, if anything, is being said on the Internet about your company.* Make sure any monitoring covers more than simply the online services. Have the service find out what's happening in the chat rooms and on the bulletin boards.

▶ *Teach yourself and the senior members of the company, especially those who will have contact with the media, how to find their way around on the Internet.* A basic browsing tutorial will help you sound smart about the online world even if you aren't.

If you're a chief executive or senior executive, don't worry too much about being out of step. Chances are, most of your rivals in the upper ranks of business are struggling with the same learning curve. But make an effort. It can have a positive influence on the image of your company if you and your senior management team are perceived to be comfortable in the online world.

And remember, online relationships with the media or anyone else are important, but they cannot take the place of one-on-one, face-to-face contact. Use online communications as a fast, effective, efficient tool to support the personal relationships you build and maintain with reporters. Reporters still consider the human touch to be the most preferable way to work their craft.

# CHAPTER 6

# The "Me" Media
## Online's Darker Side

W hat happens when cyberspace becomes not a tool of the media but a tool of nonjournalists—regular people—who use it as an interactive forum to air their beefs or to simply make fun of companies? In many ways, the growth of the chat room and the bulletin board on the Internet has created a very dangerous blind spot for companies and the public relations executives who manage their clients' public faces. It is the unexpected, and, therefore, more dangerous side of the online revolution. It is media, in that it is a channel of distribution for information, but it is not media in the traditional sense. It is, appropriately enough, "me" media—a personal form of expression published for all to see. At least when the traditional media, and even the online media, seek information about your company or write about it, there is a good chance you will know. You can see them coming. And, for the most part, the media is bound by certain ethical rules of journalism, however weakened they may be, that give you recourse if reporters get something wrong. There is some measure of protection, however porous, when dealing with an established media outlet, even if the journalist representing that outlet turns out to be a bad apple.

But there is no such protection in the "me" media, an underworld of chat rooms that allows people to exercise their rights of free speech, and where rumor and innuendo flow freely back and forth unchecked. Some of it is harmless. Some of it is not. And even more worrisome for companies, these places have become the new street corners, where private conversations take place twenty-four hours a day.

The wonderful thing—or the troubling thing depending on where you stand—is that these street-corner conversations are not so private. Anyone can join in for a minute or an hour. People can come and go as they please. And in most cases, there's no need to identify yourself. You can assume a different identity, becoming someone you've always wanted to be or someone you may have been afraid to be. It doesn't matter. Cyberspace offers a liberating degree of separation and anonymity that generates a rapid and unrestrained exchange of information and opinion. Outrageousness is fueled by an environment in which anonymity means no accountability. You can say pretty much anything you want about anyone or anything. There is no censor, no big brother, no established ethical framework that places restrictions on pronouncements, requiring them to be clean, logical, or true. Sometimes information is incorrect, or the opinion is simply nonsense. But sometimes the adage is true: Where there's smoke, there's fire. And the media sees the smoke and comes running to report the fire.

## The Pentium Chip Disaster

If ever there was a case study that illustrates the dangers of ignoring the growing influence of the cyberspace subculture, it is the Intel Corporation's Pentium chip disaster. What is most remarkable about the crisis is that it happened to Intel, a technology company that theoretically should have been more tuned in. Most people would not have been surprised if a nontechnology company had been caught not paying attention to what was being said about it online in the early 1990s. But when a leading technology company like Intel—which makes bits of the hardware that enables computers to do all the wonderful things they do, including linking with the Internet—gets tripped up by ignoring the same technological revolution that had made it a success, the lessons are obvious. You are never safe, even in your own backyard. You are possibly even more at risk because your own backyard is probably the last place you would expect to find trouble. And the road to disaster is paved with complacency.

Intel was in the middle of a $150 million brand-building advertising campaign when rumblings began in online chat rooms about flaws in its Pentium chip. The chatter began with a college professor, who went online to reveal that the chip was defective. The chip apparently caused errors when performing particularly complicated calculations. While the average person probably would never have been inconvenienced by the flaw, fear spread through online chat rooms that all calculations performed by the chip were at risk. In truth, the fear was unfounded, according to the experts. They said that most people could use the chip and never have a problem. The flaw would not affect the calculation of a monthly car payment, keeping track of household expenses, or the refinancing calculations on a house—the tasks people typically perform on their home computers. However, if you were calculating equations involving molecular weights, the sums of which run out to several decimal places, you might have a problem. One of the many jokes at the time was that the only people inconvenienced by the Pentium chip problem—rocket scientists—could probably do the calculations in their heads anyway.

Intel did at least a couple of curious things. First, it was revealed later, the company knew all about the flaw but had decided to hide the information. Second, it misjudged the growing influence of Internet chat rooms and did not react, or more precisely, reacted in a way that added fuel to the fire. Instead of stepping up and admitting the mistake, it said the defective chips really would affect only a small percentage of users and offered to replace the chip only to that group of customers. In effect, Intel committed a fatal communications blunder. It addressed the reality of the situation, not the perception. To be sure, the fact that the flaw would impact only a small percentage of users was real; but the perception among all consumers was that the chip was suspect. And besides, why should certain customers get special treatment? Everyone had paid for the chip fair and square. Did Intel mean by its limited recall offer that some customers were more important than others? It was a damaging question at a time when Intel was besieged with damaging questions.

In the meantime, the chatter online attracted the attention of some reporters. News of the flaw quickly spread through the media and suddenly, the company had a full-fledged crisis on its hands. A series of public relations blunders, all intended to downplay the problem, escalated the situation into one of the biggest catastrophes involving a reputation in recent corporate history. It lasted a month, during which time the company's stock lost 2 percent of its value. The crisis ended with Intel's chief executive officer, Andrew Grove, admitting that the company had been arrogant in its refusal to acknowledge the mistake immediately and to replace the defective parts for customers. In the end, the company launched a new advertising campaign that said simply, "We apologize."

## AOL Does the Right Thing

A lot of companies learned, or should have learned, lessons from Intel. The problem certainly made an impact on America Online (AOL), the highly successful company that is the leader in providing Internet access to millions of customers. Like Intel, AOL was a high flyer in the mid-1990s. It was leading the drive to control precious gateways to the online world, it had a young charismatic chief executive in Steve Case, and its initial public offering was destined to be a Wall Street darling before Internet companies were considered to be darlings. But like so many who have underestimated the explosive growth of the Internet, or who simply have not been able to keep up with the growth, AOL was overtaken by the demand for its services. There were too many customers and too little infrastructure to handle the demand. The AOL system became overloaded, and users frequently had great difficulty signing on and gaining access to the Internet, a privilege for which they were paying up to $30 a month as AOL subscribers. People got angry, and AOL was in trouble.

But Steve Case took the page on online crisis communications that clearly had been missing from Intel's book and did the right thing. He did not hide. Instead, he appeared in an advertising campaign designed specifically to deal with the problem. Yes, he told viewers and readers, the company had fallen behind the demand for its services and was scrambling to increase its capacity. That would probably take a few months. Sorry for the inconvenience. Thanks for your patience. Honesty, apology, contrition. What could people say? They could still be angry when their computers didn't connect to the Internet, but they couldn't say that AOL was a terrible company or that Steve Case was anything less than a straight shooter.

In fact, people are generally pretty forgiving and supportive if, in a case like this, a company and its senior executive come clean and give assurances that whatever the problem is can be fixed and will be fixed. AOL and Case won big points on the reputation front, turning a near disaster into a public relations coup. And the company is reaping the benefits today. In fact, it has come back from that potentially fatal disaster even stronger. AOL continues to be a runaway success, and the goodwill on account will not be forgotten with the next technological glitch.

Some say that if President Clinton had followed the same simple steps—honesty, apology, contrition—early on in the Monica Lewinsky scandal, it never would have escalated to the embarrassing and damaging spectacle of an impeachment hearing. But it was the President's own refusal to own up to what he did that lost him favor and credibility with the American public. He misread the public's basic test of character—they will forgive you if you're wrong but not if you're untruthful.

## Business Development Scams

So, we've seen how two companies handled such problems. But there's another danger lurking in the "me" media that falls some-

where in between media misbehavior and personal outrageousness. It is, for lack of a better term, deceitful business development.
It's really nothing new: Create a problem where none exists, then
sell your services to the victim of the crisis. In the old days, and perhaps it still goes on, some public relations consultants, eager to
generate business from clients, were known to plant bad news
about their clients with reporters or give reporters a little scuttle-
butt that could turn into potentially damaging stories. The result:
instant crisis and more business for the consultant. Indeed, in crisis
situations, consultants typically charge their clients more money,
and fear usually compels their clients to pay it.

This age-old business development tool has appeared
online, too, and it circulates through the chat rooms and bulletin
boards of the Internet. Here's an example: While working as a
media consultant, I received a telephone call one day from a
reporter who wanted to confirm that my client, a big investment
bank, had changed its stance on the implications of the year
2000, or Y2K, problem on the stock market. My client had been
fairly sanguine about the situation, saying that while there were
concerns about technological glitches in overseas markets, the
Chicken Little approach to Y2K—that the sky would fall at midnight on December 31, 1999—was simply overhyped. It was, in
effect, a story based on rumor, speculation, and feeding off the
fears of average consumers who were worried that at the
bewitching hour, elevators would stop, airplanes would fall from
the sky, and people would not be able to get their spending
money from automatic teller machines. All this because computers were not programmed to distinguish the two zeros at the end
of 2000 from those at the end of 1900. When the clock struck
midnight, a whole century of information would be lost.

This reporter claimed to have seen a report, circulated online,
that said the opposite—my client was now saying the fears about
Y2K were real and that Armageddon was nigh. Not only that, the
reporter said, the bulletin board report, written as if it were a news
story, claimed that my client was predicting computer glitches that
would wipe out account records at banks and other financial institu-

tions, forever eliminating people's retirement savings, college funds, insurance policies, pension funds, bank and brokerage accounts, mortgage records, and everything else that people need to survive. In effect, Y2K would make the world broke in the blink of an eye.

The report, which had originated somewhere in Europe, had not been picked up by any other media. But if it were as apocalyptic as this reporter said, it soon would be. My first step was to try to track down the report. It wasn't easy, but with a little searching, I succeeded. Sure enough, the report was written to look like a news story—or perhaps a cross between a news story and a press release—though there were a couple of curious aspects to it that piqued my curiosity. First, the name of the contact for more information was also the name of the person quoted in the story as the expert. Second, the spokesman's comments seemed to indicate that he not only agreed with my client but was actually involved in some way with my client's Y2K efforts.

In the meantime, I called the client. No, he told me, there had been no change in the company's outlook for Y2K. And no, he had not seen or heard about this report, which was strange because he is closely tuned in to what is being said about him and the company on all frequencies. And if anything is wrong—if he is misquoted—he blows a gasket. Reporters who have been on the losing end of an argument with this executive will never make the same mistake twice. And finally, he had never heard of the spokesman named in the release, either as a journalist or as someone with whom he or his company had done business.

We did some research. Using data bases and contacts in the technology side of the business, we were able to track down the mystery man. It turns out he was a Y2K consultant, specializing in contracting himself out to companies that were having problems with the remediation of their systems. As a business development tool, he had used the technology that allows the creation of documents that look like the real thing—news stories or press releases— and developed a credible-looking professional report. Knowing the power and broad influence of the online chat rooms and bulletin boards, he had used them to disseminate his message. To those who were cruising the Net, not paying attention to where they were online, the report looked like a perfectly legitimate document from a reliable source. By including the name of a well-known company and one of its well-known executives in the copy, he added even more credibility and attracted more attention. And by claiming that this well known executive from a well-known company had made a dramatic change in his point of view, he was sure to raise eyebrows and maybe even create news that would get his name in the paper. The fact that he intimated he had a relationship with my client was icing on the cake. This guy was pretty good, though his self-promotional motivation was pretty predictable.

And this was not the first time he had pulled such a stunt. Our research showed that he had made a habit of linking himself with important people or companies and producing reports that looked like the real thing. And by floating them out in the random, unregulated universe of cyberspace, he left only a very faint trail to be followed by those who would seek to shut him down. In the end, we were able to trace him only so far before he disappeared into thin air. We're almost certain he'll be back, though perhaps in a different form, using a different name and exploiting a different company. But the scam will be the same.

The annoyance factor of the incident was only part of the problem. The report and the media attention it generated forced my client's hand. On his behalf, we had to issue a news release denying the report and reiterating my client's stance on the issue, even though the credibility of the report was suspect. My client worried that he looked dumb, responding to something so foolish. But it was an exercise in correcting misinformation. Since we couldn't find the source, we had to do it ourselves. The reporters who read our release and called to ask about the report were equally mystified. Some had been able to track it down. Others could not. Those who saw it wondered who the author was and why he would waste his time making up such a story. When told of the connection between what he wrote and what he did for a living, it became clear.

For companies, this incident certainly highlights a problem. But it also means trouble for the media. It is clear that there are people out there who are impersonating reporters—and companies, for that matter—and generating false news and opinion. The average reader, wandering around unprotected in the online environment, doesn't know the difference between a real story and a phony one. Technology has made it possible for news forgeries to look very real, very convincing. And there is very little anyone can do about it. There are inherent dangers in imposing regulations on the Internet limiting the spread of such information, but some measure of control is clearly needed. While companies are at risk in that their names are being used for illicit purposes, it's the media who suffer more. The media is already suffering from a credibility problem, and fake work of this sort throws their credibility into furthur doubt. And it is the consumer who suffers the most. Had the phony report involving my client been of a material nature, people may have made decisions based on the information it contained. If they had lost money, they would have blamed the company and the media that carried the story. Since the author couldn't be found and probably wouldn't care, who would take the heat? The companies and any media that happened to be standing nearby.

## The Wild Internet Environment

Online antics aren't always serious or material. But they can be damaging and expensive. We all remember when, in the early days of the Internet, some enterprising individuals, who were familiar with the way the online universe worked, gobbled up the likely Web site names of major companies, registered them in their own names, then held the companies hostage until they paid for the rights to buy back their own names. Some companies paid tens of thousands of dollars to these cyber bandits, creating what may have been the earliest form of e-commerce. Come to think of it, those entrepreneurs may have been the first and only people to figure out how to actually make money in the online universe. Now, of course, companies go to great lengths to ensure that they own their Web site names and several related names, including common misspellings.

With the extortion loophole pretty much closed, online pranksters now are turning to less lucrative but more creative methods to jerk companies' chains. And they are wreaking havoc with companies' reputations on the Internet. In early 1999, my office was alerted to a peculiar and unexpected problem: Some joker had linked PaineWebber's corporate site on the Web to a pornography site. By leaving out a single character in the company's Web address, Internet users  heading for financial information about the firm found themselves on a home page with scantily clad women offering all sorts of favors. Instead of getting information on mutual funds, unsuspecting online customers found themselves with sneak peak pictorials of surgically enhanced women, eagerly awaiting their calls over a toll-free number that flashed on the screen. Now while some may have not been ruffled by the discovery—Wall Street is still trying hard to overcome its image as a macho, chauvinistic culture—most were startled. And the typographical change that made the connection to the rogue Web site was so small and subtle that many could not figure out what was going on. Some people who carefully reentered the proper address for the firm figured they had been seeing things when the real site popped up as expected.

While the jokes about the juxtaposition of the conservative, 120-year-old brokerage firm with the racy Web site swirled, the firm took the problem very seriously. In fact, its swift and aggressive action to shut down the offending site became a precedent-setting case. The firm received an injunction against the hackers who had devised the deception, and the court closed up their shop. The case was interesting in that it pointed out that this type of freedom of expression was not permissible because it was potentially harmful to the company's reputation and business. In effect, the court ruled that the site could cause the firm to lose business. The hackers' actions were no longer considered a silly prank. They were endangering people's money and livelihoods. Still, the incident and the case attracted the attention of the media, and while the responsible media fairly represented the more serious legal and business issues associated with the problem, others simply couldn't resist making fun of the whole peculiar situation.

An important point is that the discovery of the so-called rogue Web site was no accident. And herein lies a lesson for all firms who have public Web sites used by their customers, shareholders, investment analysts, and the media. The firm, like many large companies, had been forced to hire an Internet monitoring service to scan for everything from misuse of the brand name to misinformation about the firm spreading through chat rooms and bulletin boards to links that could damage the firm's brand and reputation. Originally, the service had been contracted through the company's legal department, as a way to monitor trademark misuse and any attempt by people inside or outside to disseminate unauthorized investment information or solicit business in ways that contradicted policy. But the effort quickly spread to encompass all communications issues.

## Developing an Online Policy

So what should companies be doing in the "me" media generation of online communications? The first thing to do is understand what's happening out there. If you have never visited a chat room or a bulletin board, take a look. There is something for everyone. But remember, it is a world where nothing is as it appears. Participants are disguised. There is no credibility whatsoever.

The second thing to do is commission an audit of your corporate Web site if you have one. Have someone check to make sure you own as many of the reasonably expected derivations of your company's name as possible. And be careful. You might be surprised at how adept cyber pranksters are at the subtleties of the piracy of website names. In addition, check to make sure that your site is not linked in any way to other inappropriate sites. This doesn't mean only pornography sites. There have been cases where either by mistake, or through some twisted sense of humor, competitors have had their sites hot-linked. Imagine the chagrin of the senior executive who clicks onto a portion of his company's site only to be transported instantly to the competing site of his arch rival.

The third thing to do is design and enforce an Internet or online policy. Many companies already have strict e-mail policies prohibiting the creation and distribution of inappropriate messages, including obscene language and pornographic information. So strict are many companies that people lose their jobs for violating the policy. In one celebrated case, a high-ranking research analyst at a major Wall Street firm was dismissed for forwarding pornographic material via e-mail to his colleagues. He had not generated the material himself or downloaded it from another site. It had been sent to him by an acquaintance outside the company, and he had forwarded it. Many companies also have internal monitoring systems by which they keep track of e-mail traffic. Using key words that will tip them off to illegal or inappropriate messaging, these monitors have greatly restricted and reduced the flow of nonessential, nonbusiness e-mail on company systems. And while employees feel they have no freedom—big brother is watching—companies consider this surveillance essential to reducing liability for discrimination and harassment cases. This practice will become increasingly important as e-mail continues to grow as a popular communications tool. Consider these statistics from a recent PaineWebber Internet Analysis study: The number of daily e-mails in the United States now exceeds the number of pieces of traditional mail delivered by more than 30 to 1. And the number of e-mails is expected to surpass the number of telephone calls on a daily basis over the next couple of years.

But an online policy should go beyond e-mail. It can be incorporated under a broader communications policy. Many companies have policies that prohibit their employees from discussing the affairs of the company with any outside media—print, broadcast, online, or other—without approval from the public relations department. The goal of such policies is not to create a police state but to try to control the messages the company distributes and keep those messages consistent. Thoughtful companies appeal to their employees' common sense for compliance, reminding them that they probably do not want to be on the hook as a spokesperson for the company without being prepared. It is understood that employees could lose their jobs if they violate the policy. And while it is impossible to regulate what people say—whether it's around the dinner table or in an online chat room—it is important to let your employees know that you take every form of public corre- spondence about the company very seriously. Will it protect you from gripes? No. But it will put in place a structure that will help you manage the day-to-day flow of communications and may give support in the time of a crisis.

## Using an Online Monitoring Service

In addition to establishing policy, another step is to hire an online monitoring service, not only for legal issues but for broader com- munications issues as well. Tracking or monitoring systems enlisted by legal departments usually focus only on Web sites; they rarely scan online news services, chat rooms, bulletin boards, Webzines, or the other countless online media vehicles. That's because the legal department's concerns are much narrower than those of the communications people. The legal department cares mainly about whether the company's name is being misused, if others are using the company's name illegally to conduct business, or if the name is being used in libelous or slanderous ways. There is no question that these concerns are vital to the well-being of the company. But if they are the only focus of an online monitoring effort, your com- pany is going to miss the kind of chatter that hurt Intel, the shady dealers who misrepresented themselves and my financial client's name and, perhaps, even the cyber pranksters who linked PaineWebber's Web site to the pornography site.

When choosing a monitoring service, make sure there is some upfront counseling by your company's communications people and, ideally, a public relations professional to oversee the monitoring effort. Many big companies set it up this way. They will contract the job to a public relations agency that has a spe- cialty in online communications. The agency will work with the client company to determine what issues are important, those that may be harmful, and those that are of general interest to the firm. They will come up with a list of key words, red flags that will alert the monitors to smoke that may indicate fire. The agency and the client will also work together to determine the scope of the monitoring project—which outlets should be included, what browsers to use, how often the monitoring is to be done. Make sure that when determining the scope, the monitoring goes beyond a simple clipping service that retrieves news articles. You should not be too worried about tracking the recognized media—if they publish something noteworthy about your company, you'll hear about it. The real goal is to keep a close eye on the "me" media. Sweep those chat rooms and bulletin boards. Keep track of what those independent publishers may be saying about you. In addition, this part of the process should also put in place a quick-response plan if the monitoring turns up a potentially dangerous or damaging piece of information or chat group issue. It should be linked to whatever crisis communications plan you have in place, if any, because a crisis that begins online will not be contained there for long in this environment.

The agency, in turn, will subcontract the monitoring portion of the job to a monitoring company such as e-watch. While this is the purely technical part, it is important that it is done properly and with appropriate scope. The agency should work closely with the monitoring service to cover all the bases, and in particular, avoid the blind spots. Again, while it is important to sweep the recognized news services, the real goal is to dig deep into the less structured sites—the petrie dishes for problems.

Will these methods provide total coverage? Absolutely not. Because of the countless sources of information on the Internet and the fact that people and entities can exist online anonymously, it is virtually impossible to have bulletproof protection. But such monitoring can do a great deal to help you be prepared. It will certainly make you better informed. And it will give you the kind of early warning protection that may give you time to prepare an appropriate response in the event of a problem. Remem-

ber, in the modern media environment, things happen with light-
ning speed. Information travels quickly to many places around
the world. If you can have a few hours warning that trouble is
brewing, it will give you a better chance of making a reasoned
response. Those of you who have been in the middle of a communications crisis are aware of how difficult it is to keep your
head and make sense when surrounded by chaos. The amount of
time, no matter how small, that an effective monitoring system
can provide you can make the difference between saving or
blowing the reputation of the company.

The companies that have adapted early to this online environment and taken steps to manage it are already enjoying the
benefits of being plugged in. Such companies are perceived to be
on the leading edge, responsive, and responsible. The companies
that have lagged behind are finding it difficult to catch up
because the online world is moving too quickly for everyone to
keep pace. An "online year" is only about three months long,
meaning that successful Internet strategies must go from concept
to market in three months. Most of corporate America is still
scrambling to keep up with this time compression phenomenon.
Companies are paying in the image department for being late. As
the saying goes, forewarned is forearmed. It pays to be well
armed in this environment because huge sections of the online
word are unregulated. They are truly new frontiers, wild places
where there are no rules, no laws, and no one to protect the
rights and good names of people and companies.

## Summary of Trends

▶ *The growth of the Internet has seen the advent of the
"me" media environment where individuals use chat
rooms, bulletin boards, and other online vehicles to publish their own personal opinions.* These venues have
become the new street corners where conversations
flow freely.

▶ *The characteristics of the "me" media are distinct from other media, including online media.* The environment is made up of individuals who do not belong to entities that operate under ethical guidelines. There is no recourse against them.

▶ *The "me" media operates in a wild environment.* There are no rules and regulations. There is no accountability. Outrageousness is encouraged, anonymity preferred. The freedom and separation of the environment provide protection for the participants.

▶ *The "Wild West" mentality of the "me" media attracts scam artists.* These people use technology to present themselves as credible and work their schemes from the relative safety of the ever-expanding online universe.

▶ *The lack of accountability of the "me" media environment creates a credibility problem for both companies and the media.* For companies, tracking and squelching incorrect information or opinion is difficult because of the anonymity of the sources. The media suffers because there is a continuous blurring of the line between reliable and unreliable information.

▶ *Pranksters are taking advantage of technology to annoy companies, and the pranks can have serious consequences for companies' reputations and images.*

## Lessons for Companies

▶ *Plug in.* Find out what's going on. You cannot afford to be ignorant of the trends.

▶ *Conduct an audit of your online capabilities.* Do you have complete control of your domain? Are there inappropriate or damaging links to and from your corporate Web site? If so, it's time to fix your system.

▶ *Develop and implement an online policy that goes beyond e-mail.* Make sure it encompasses all communications issues. Make it appeal to the common sense of employees. Explain the dangers of unauthorized contact with the media. And give the policy some teeth.

▶ *Develop an online monitoring strategy that goes beyond narrow issues of a strictly legal nature.* Ideally, have an outside agency act as a middleman between you and the monitoring service. Carefully choose the scope and content of the monitoring effort. Go deep, beyond the online news services, to the chat rooms and bulletin boards.

▶ *Develop a quick-response plan for online crises.* Link it to your overall crisis communications plan.

▶ *Be aggressive when you have been wronged online.* The rules, at least from a legal point of view, are still being written about what is acceptable and what is not. Since there is no formal regulation, don't be afraid to set precedent. Your company will benefit just for trying. You will be perceived as understanding the online world and being comfortable enough with it to rattle some chains.

▶ *Move quickly.* An online year lasts only three months. By tomorrow, you already will have lost more time than you realize.

# CHAPTER 7

# The Reluctant Media Darling
## Lessons From Wall Street

The day Robert Rubin resigned as secretary of the treasury for the Clinton administration in the spring of 1999, I got a telephone call from a producer for the "CBS Evening News" with Dan Rather, who wanted the chairman of PaineWebber to appear that night to discuss how Rubin's resignation would affect the markets in the United States and overseas, the political landscape, and the nation as a whole. Alas, I told the producer, even though he had called only moments after the news of the resignation hit the wires, the chairman had already received eight requests to appear on television and had committed to an appearance on CNN's "Moneyline News Hour" with Lou Dobbs.

In the car on the way to the CNN studios in Manhattan that evening, the chairman, Donald Marron, and I spoke about the remarkable media coverage Secretary Rubin's resignation had generated. A full news conference at the White House, with the president speaking and Rubin handing over the reins of the treasury to Larry Sommers, broadcast live on all the major networks and several cable channels. And an endless stream of requests throughout the day for our firm, and presumably others, to offer up spokespeople—if not the chairman, then someone else—to talk about the impact of Rubin's move. "It's amazing that the resignation of a treasury secretary has so much broad interest," Marron mused. "The fact that it's a media event tells you a lot about what's happening."

He was absolutely right. And, in fact, he and Lou Dobbs discussed the point on the program that night. They could not remember a time in this country's history when the resignation of a senior treasury official had generated so much attention among so many people. The national obsession with Wall Street and investing had made the resignation of the treasury secretary big news to a lot of people, something that would not have been true a few years ago. Rubin, along with the chairman of the Federal Reserve, Alan Greenspan, had become among the most watched personalities in America. Their influence on the financial markets, which in the recent past held the interest of only a small percentage of people, was now felt by every person with a 401(k) plan or an online trading account.

If someone had told Rubin and Greenspan a few years ago that they would be media stars, they probably would have been skeptical. Yet they are. CNBC has even taken a satirical, though friendly, jab at the troll-like Greenspan with a regular feature called the "Briefcase Indicator." The tongue-in-cheek feature claims that Americans can get an idea of whether Greenspan plans to raise or lower interest rates by the thickness of his briefcase. Film footage shows Greenspan leaving his Washington office with a briefcase under his arm. The camera then zooms in on the case, showing it either bulging with papers or relatively empty and slim. A full case, the completely unscientific theory says, indicates a raising of rates; a thin case means no action or a lowering of rates.

The glare, serious and otherwise, on Rubin and Greenspan also shines brightly on Wall Street for exactly the same reasons. The growth of individual investment during the 1990s has created a nation of Americans for whom investing is not simply a pastime, it is becoming a necessity. Wall Street is no longer the closed environment of the past. It is no longer a club, or if it is, it has millions of new members, most of whom have joined only in the last few years.

## A Shy Violet Exposed

The remarkable transformation of Wall Street from a shy violet into a media darling provides lessons for all companies in all industries on managing the new business media environment. In effect, Wall Street firms, even those that have been around a long time, have gone through the same pains that new public companies suffer in, adapting to a whole new set of audiences and demands. Wall Street firms can no longer simply talk to themselves or to each other—the same way small companies can't. They need to learn to talk to more people about more things and in different ways.

The Wall Street experience has been one of sweeping, overnight change. A decade ago, most investment companies lived in a closed media environment. The income invested in the financial markets was largely discretionary, which meant most of the players were large and wealthy. The investment community was small and exclusive, made up of institutions, corporations, and a few wealthy individuals. As PaineWebber's Marron paints it, the modern investing environment has gone through three decades of profound change. The 1970s was the decade of the institution, when pension funds grew large and used the finan-cial markets to fund that growth. The 1980s, by contrast, was the decade of the corporation, during which time American companies looked for capital to grow and become competitive globally. They also turned to the financial markets for help. The 1990s, as we have said, has been the decade of the individual who is assuming responsibility for his or her own financial health and future and is turning to stock-market investments as the solution. This shift in responsibility has reshaped the financial markets in ways that were unimagined a decade ago.

## The Decade of the Individual

The unprecedented bull market run of the late 1990s, fueled mainly by the inflow of money from individuals, proved Marron's thesis. With the move by companies away from defined benefit plans to defined contribution plans and the growing concerns about the long-term reliability of Social Security, investing has become an essential part of financial and retirement planning, not simply an exercise for wealthy speculators, institutions, and companies. Studies commissioned by PaineWebber and conducted by The Gallup Organization show that fully one-third of Americans now consider themselves to be investors, with $10,000 or more in investable assets and many holding 401(k) plans, mutual funds, and IRAs. In effect, Marron said, the shift has created a nation of pension fund managers, few of whom are qualified for the job.

Add to this the demographic trends and the phenomenon is expected to continue for at least another decade. As the members of the baby boom generation prepare for retirement, they are transforming themselves from spenders into savers. More sophisticated than their parents about investing and increasingly comfortable with the technology that allows them to cruise around the world on the Internet looking for opportunities to trade online, these people are pouring billions of dollars into the financial markets. Their goal: to ensure their financial security at retirement and preempt the need to rely on a Social Security system that seems doomed to fail if some sort of reform is not pursued in the very near future.

This shift has created a huge interest in Wall Street and the financial markets. And in many ways, it has created a dangerous euphoria, sometimes bordering on hysteria, that has been fueled by the bull market. There is a feeling among many investors, particularly young ones, that they are invincible when it comes to playing the stock market. For many who have been investors for only a few years, the concept of a major correction or a bear market is inconceivable. Despite warnings from those who have seen the bad and the good, many of these investors continue to overextend themselves and expect unrealistic returns from their investments.

Wall Street, in the meantime, has had to walk a fine line. Eager to share in and profit from the new excitement surrounding investing, the Street has tried to manage the expectations of investors, particularly those young high flyers who think that the market has nowhere to go but up and successful stock picking can be done with their eyes closed. It is a peculiar conundrum for firms: How do they encourage people to invest while reminding them that there is no guarantee of success? Indeed, in a down market, investors lose the money they have been counting on for their children's college education or for their retirement.

## Consolidation

Complicating the situation even further has been widespread consolidation among the big firms on the Street and the emergence of hundreds of new companies in many different forms. If you look at the list of major stock brokerage companies of ten years ago, almost every one in the top ten has either changed hands, gone out of business, or merged with another entity. Only Merrill Lynch and PaineWebber remain as independent, national full-service companies.

There are several reasons for this trend. First, everyone in financial services recognized that this was the business in which to be, so the market became very crowded overnight. Second, to reach the critical mass needed to gain as much market share as possible in this growing market, big companies decided they needed to get bigger. Those companies wanted to go global and needed the size to tackle overseas markets. Third, technology opened up a whole new business. Discounters and online brokerages came and went. In the early 1990s, the prediction was that by the turn of the century, there would be thousands of discounters, and the full-service business would be dead. As it turned out, at the end of the century, there are three big discounters that control 80 percent of the discount market. And, curiously enough, the leader of these, Charles Schwab, has built more than three hundred offices across the country, giving it more bricks and mortar that many of the traditional full-service brokerages.

## Growth of Online Trading

And then there's the world of online trading, in which individuals can use any number of Internet trading services to manage their own portfolios. Most big firms, including the discounters, would argue that what people do online from their living rooms is day trading, not investing. Investing, by their definition, involves research and portfolio management and all the things that people need when planning their futures. It is not, they contend, playing the "market up, market down" game. Still, millions of people a day sign on to their computers and trade online. Whether they make any money over time remains to be seen. But uncertainty doesn't stop them from trying.

The upshot of all these developments is that the Wall Street world of the 1990s became a noisy and chaotic place. Brands came and went. Old brands disappeared or popped up in new guises. New brands arrived, grew, died, or were taken over. Products, too, came and went, some successful, some not. New investors, faced with growing responsibility for their own financial well-being, were seduced by the apparent easy money of the bull market. They wanted to know what this investing stuff was all about. They were unsophisticated, but enthusiastic—too much so, it may turn out if they get caught unprepared in a future market downturn. They wanted information, opinion. They wanted products that were customized to their needs. And they wanted the convenience of technology to make it all easier.

But, for the most part, they were confused. When they looked for advice, they were faced with the question, Whom should we trust? Most of these people didn't recognize any brand names on the Street, even those that had been around for decades. These were people whose brand knowledge was pretty much Coca-Cola and Ford, and to a growing extent Nike and Microsoft. But Morgan Stanley Dean Witter? Bear Stearns? Smith Barney? Some of them may have remembered some of the old advertising slogans— "When E.F. Hutton talks, people listen"—but many were too young to have been around at the time. And besides, if they went to look for E.F. Hutton in the phone book, it isn't there. Some of them turned into do-it-yourselfers, which fueled the growth of online trading. But the market had become so fragmented that it was impossible for even the most experienced observers to make sense of it all.

It is also worth remembering what was at the core of all this activity, interest, and commerce: money. And money is a very emotional issue for most people. The adage of old-style gamblers and investors, "never bet more than you can afford to lose" was lost on this group, which was unsophisticated in the ways of the market and convinced that returns would always keep rising. It's all they knew. There is a wonderful story, told by a Wall Street chief executive, that illustrates the point about the emotional power of money. While at a dinner party with a number of prominent guests, the discussion turned first to sex. One of the men at the table, well plied with wine, was rambling on about his sex life which was pretty entertaining. He left out no detail, including as much graphic description as mixed, polite company would allow, and told about his exploits in a deliciously slow pace that had his fellow guests hanging on to every word. Then, abruptly, the discussion turned to money. And in an unguarded moment, someone asked the man who described his sex life how much money he made. The conversation stopped dead. The guest was incensed. There was no more laughter. The host, sensing trouble, quickly changed the subject, and the conversation continued. At the end of the party, the woman who had asked the guest the question about money took him aside to apologize. "I had no idea I had offended you when I asked about money," she told him. "After all, you seemed happy to tell us every detail about your sex life." In a huff, the man replied: "It doesn't matter what I say about sex, my money is nobody's business." Which is a roundabout way of saying that in the new environment in which Wall Street found itself in the 1990s, the underlying dynamic that fueled it all was an extremely emotional element of human nature.

The combination was like a powder keg with a short fuse. There was a lot of money to be made and lost—though new investors seldom thought about the latter. It was the type of double-edge thrill that gives people goosebumps—the same way viewers of the movie "Wall Street" felt. This investing thing was new, a little mysterious, a little sexy. There was a chance to be rich—richer than most people could have imagined. But there was also the prospect of losing it all. There was a strong dose of the gambler's mentality thrown into an equation that was basically driven by people's need to secure their financial futures.

## The Changing Media Coverage

This thrill—the possibility of big gains and the danger of big losses—changed the media's interest in Wall Street, too. A decade before, the media covering Wall Street was appropriately small and almost exclusively print. Only a few outlets mattered, among them *The Wall Street Journal, The New York Times, Forbes, Fortune, Business Week* and to an extent *Financial World.* To say that CNN's "Moneyline," "Wall Street Week" or "Nightly Business Report" had broad reach was a stretch. The coverage was pretty dull, for the most part, and directed at the executives who ran the companies that the papers covered. At that time, there was no effort to cater to individual investors, mainly because they had yet to emerge as a force in the markets. Wall Street firms lived in veritable anonymity, some even struggling to get their names in print. Several did during the 1980s boom in investment banking, when big deals made big money. But the audience for these stories was limited. The firms involved in the financing were far from becoming household names.

*The New York Times* business news coverage of the early 1990s reflected this perfectly. When I arrived as an editor at the paper's West 43rd Street office in Manhattan in the early 1990s, the business section was gray and uninteresting. The articles were ponderous. There were few faces with the stories, and any that appeared were those of pudgy white executives in white shirts and ties looking smug. The section, while it provided a good helping of solid information every day, had no personality. The writing was bland. The story lineup was predictable. The section was still talking to the corporations, which in the 1980s drove the markets. It had yet to talk to the individuals, the emerging market drivers of the 1990s.

In the meantime, personal finance magazines were growing like weeds, as were personal finance newsletters. *Money* magazine, *Worth, Your Money, Kiplinger's,* and many others were all attracting readers and attention. *The Wall Street Journal* had even ventured into the arena with *Smart Money* and had put some of the paper's senior journalists in charge of the new magazine. It was clear that something was happening out there, and average

Americans were beginning to demand more business news than what was being offered by the traditional outlets, including the business paper of record, *The Wall Street Journal.*

And while the online world had not yet caught fire, many of the business media outlets were experimenting with Web sites and editorial content. The issue: How could they provide content to the Web site without cannibalizing their print products? It was a concern that became moot within a few years.

## Dressing Up the Gray Lady

So, back at *The New York Times,* the senior editors had clearly heard the rumblings, too. Enter John Geddes who was hired as the business editor of the *Times* in 1994. Almost immediately the section came to life. Geddes, a personable fellow with good ideas and collegial management style, had arrived at the *Times* from *The Wall Street Journal* and had spent a brief period in private business, so he had the journalistic and business credentials to impress. But he had more than that. It was apparent that he, too, had seen the shift to the individual investor and had begun hearing the new demands they were creating for business news. More important, at *the Times,* Geddes had the vision and easy style that allowed him to break, or at least bend, some of the traditions of the paper to do what he thought was necessary with the section. For those who don't know, changing things—any thing—at *The New York Times* is next to impossible. Traditions run so deep, and the processes are so ingrained that even small changes require the force and conviction needed to move mountains. This is not in any way a criticism. After all, the *Times* is the most influential newspaper in the United States, perhaps in the world. It knows how to do things properly and successfully. Understandably, it guards its successful formula closely.

Yet Geddes was able to bring his skills and personality to bear. With the support of senior management, he set about doing what many thought impossible—make the *Times'* business section a good read for more people. The transformation was so swift and effective, it made many heads spin. He bent a lot of rules, some radically. For example, he played around with the *Business Day* masthead to make it more visually appealing. At the *Times*, visual appeal had never topped the priority list—remember, this is a newspaper that only began using color in the 1990s, and even then after much agonizing by senior management and much griping by the traditionalists, both inside and outside the paper. Yet, there was Geddes' work, every morning, looking jaunty and cheeky. The *Business Day* masthead became almost a logo in itself, incorporating everything from computer mice and floppy disks to printer connection cables and electric plugs. Readers didn't know quite what to think at first, but they sort of liked what they were seeing. Was the *Times* actually becoming fun?

Yet the changes were more than cosmetic. Geddes improved the story mix to reflect the growing demand from readers for in-depth information. The daily display feature article of the dress page of the section was usually an interesting look at how a company had solved a problem or not. The feature contained information as well as lessons and insight. Spot news coverage became more competitive, too. While the *Times*, as a general interest daily, had no intention of becoming the business paper of record like *The Wall Street Journal*, there was credibility to be gained by being competitive on breaking news stories. Nothing attracts readers like scoops—and if the *Times* could be competitive more often than not, more readers would see that the new business section, to steal a line from a car ad, was not their father's business section. During the early 1990s, reporters went head-to-head with their rivals at the *Journal*. The news desks were on fire many a night with breaking, competitive stories about big mergers and acquisitions.

Meanwhile, the Sunday business section was also changing. It began to look a lot like a personal finance magazine. There were columns on markets, investment advice, mutual funds. The cover stories also were lesson-driven, containing profiles of issues or personalities that gave readers more insight into the way the world of business worked, both good and bad. Those who read the *Times* every day of the week got the best of all worlds—hard news and insightful features spinning off the news in the daily section and personal finance information in the Sunday paper. And the readers liked what they were getting. After getting over the initial shock of the changes— faithful readers typically enjoyed the fact that the *Times* almost never changed, and if it did, it did so only slightly—the readers started to respond to the new approach. The business section was more readable and less intimidating than *The Wall Street Journal*, especially for new investors. And because of the *Times* name and reputation, readers were reassured that the information they were getting came from a reliable source. Geddes' vision was becoming realized. And the naysayers, who had been getting progressively quieter, pretty much shut up all together.

At the same time, Floyd Norris, the *Times'* business guru, had undertaken a huge and extremely crucial project to attract and interest individual investors: the daily stock tables. Typically acres of gray agate type, the stock tables were hard to read, hard to follow, and pretty confusing for new investors. Even more important, new investors wanted more information about mutual funds and other investment products that most newspapers didn't follow. In addition, with the rise of the NASDAQ market, whose members are typically small and midsize companies, many of them technology based, there was growing demand to have those listings included along with the traditional listings of the New York Stock Exchange and the American Stock Exchange. To further complicate matters, there was the advent of technology, the world was growing smaller. There was a growing demand for more information about financial markets overseas where some of these new investors were testing the waters.

In a nutshell, the task was to provide a much wider range of customized information than ever before without consuming so much space that the newspaper would have to print an entirely separate section of stock tables. Norris accomplished the task by coming up with a formula that provided a lot of information in an understandable, usable form. Critics such as William O'Neill, owner and publisher the California business paper, *Investor's Business Daily*, say that the stock tables in publications like the *Times* and the *Journal* are meaningless because they provide no analysis. *IBD's* stock tables already contain analytical information using O'Neill's successful investing methods. He offers this alternative presentation to his paper's 200,000 readers. Still, what Norris accomplished at the *Times* was a great feat. It was not, in journalistic terms, a choice assignment. It was not sexy or high profile. But it was essential to the paper's transformation into a friendlier, more effective source of news and information for the growing number of individual investors.

## Responding to the New Investors

So, Wall Street companies were faced with a stiff challenge. The growing mass appeal of investing had turned their world, and indeed the entire financial services world, from an exclusive, clubby game into a consumer business. And Wall Street has been thrust into the spotlight. The media, responding to the needs of this new group of investors, set their sights on finding out more about these peculiar companies that for years had quietly made a big business out of turning money into more money. Corporate chief financial officers were no longer the only people interested in stock market activity or the earnings of securities firms. Suddenly, the Beard-stown Ladies were the hottest stock pickers in the nation, and their books more popular than those by any Wall Street tycoon.

For many Wall Street firms, the attention was overwhelming. Many did not know what to do. So many different audiences wanted so much information so much faster than ever before. For many of these firms, calls from the media had been as a rare as hen's teeth. And in a crisis, the number of people who cared was so small that problems rarely went beyond a limited audience. So even when things went wrong, it was no big deal—or at least it was no big deal to most people.

The smart firms figured out the new situation quickly. They took their leads from other consumer companies and learned about things like marketing, communications, and public relations. Most of these firms knew about and used advertising. But they realized that the demands of these new investors for insight and advice went far beyond what they could deliver through advertising. And these firms were aware that the credibility of advertising had been declining for some time. Besides, the real issue was the media. It had become the main source of information and opinion for these investors, and it was essential to become part of the new process.

One of the best examples of how a Wall Street firm recognized and reacted to these changes occurred at PaineWebber. In the mid-1990s, the firm had a very small public relations operation. It was staffed by five relatively junior people whose main job was to handle any incoming telephone calls from the media and help out with any crisis that came along. As a support mechanism, the firm had an outside public relations agency on retainer to handle the serious situations with the serious media, such as *The Wall Street Journal*. There was little proactive effort to build the profile of the firm, its products and services, or its senior management. In effect, the in-house public relations function had been back-officed. It reported to the advertising and marketing director and was considered the weak sister of the group.

For years, the setup had been perfectly adequate and, for the most part, reflected the norm on Wall Street. There really had not been any need for much more. The advertising effort handled the firm's brand identity, and the marketing department took care of offering sales support to the brokers. The media were viewed as annoyances that had to be dealt with when it called. It had never been a major channel through which the company's messages could be distributed or its image enhanced.

But with the rise of the individual investor, which brought new demands for information, and the resulting increase in media attention, it became clear to the firm that a stronger public relations effort not only was necessary but also could afford a strategic and competitive advantage. The commitment was made by senior management to develop a strong public relations capability in-house with the experienced personnel and resources to do the job right.

## Setting Up an In-House PR Capability

The recruiting began in 1995 and by the end of 1999, the public relations group—renamed the corporate communications department—consisted of more than twenty professionals. The department included: media relations, which included online communications, investor relations, internal or executive communications, and a unit dedicated to proactive support for the firm's retail brokerage network. In addition, corporate communications included the firm's diversity initiative. There was no longer a need for an outside public relations agency to speak on behalf of the firm. The group used agencies for specific projects only. Most important, the group no longer reported to advertising and marketing—it reported directly to the senior management of the company. It had the direct access to top management it needed to do the job properly.

PaineWebber boosted its image almost immediately. The firm began to speak with a single, consistent voice. It spoke in messages that reflected its strategic business objectives. And it spoke through its own people, not through outsiders. The media appreciated this for two reasons. First, they knew the internal group had access to the senior executives of the company and therefore the information they were receiving came from the top. Second, an inhouse spokesperson is perceived to have more of a vested interest in how the company is seen by the public. He or she is less likely to be dismissive of reporters and less likely to be obscure. Remember, an inhouse spokesperson wants an issue or a problem to be resolved quickly and quietly, unlike some outside consultants who make a living by generating crisis.

The corporate communications department started to build relationships with the key media for both the professionals in the group and the senior executives of the firm. This sounds more difficult than it was. They had breakfasts, lunches, casual meetings, and briefings with reporters. They put names and faces together for the first time in a long time. Remember that despite the growth of online services and the media's growing use of Internet technology as a news gathering tool, nothing is as effective in building relationships as face-to-face contacts. The move was also educational for the senior people. They began to hear, in venues outside the heat of battle, what issues interested reporters. The company began to get a sense of the reporters' agendas, the types of trends they saw influencing the industry, and ultimately, the news that the industry would make. The relationship-building process, which is an ongoing process, was our way not only of getting out our messages but also of getting some intelligence about what the other side was doing. Remember the lesson from the online media world and the "me" media: Forewarned is forearmed.

We also incorporated the online media into our communications mix. On the firm's corporate Web site, we developed a resource center and virtual newsroom for reporters to use. We hired an online media specialist to develop and maintain the site, and we hired an outside agency to help us with comprehensive monitoring, not only of the online news services but also of chat rooms and bulletin boards.

## Making News and Telling Your Story

In addition, the firm started generating its own news. It began to build the profile of the company from within, not simply let others define it based on how the firm reacted to events. We called the effort "evening the pile." The phrase referred to the traditional measure of public relations success—the thickness of the pile of daily newspaper clippings that mentioned the company's name. Our task at PaineWebber was to even the clips, which in 1996 were pretty heavily weighted on the negative side. Anyone who wanted to know about the company and checked the clipping files for reference would think that PaineWebber never did anything but get into trouble.

The news-generating effort at PaineWebber unfolded on many fronts. We improved the lines of communication throughout the company to gain access to the good things the business units were doing. In a company of nearly 20,000 employees, there were a lot of good stories. Through our improved relations with the media and their interest in learning more about the company, we were able to get some of these stories into the papers. That was pretty much basic public relations. We showcased our senior executives and the firm's growth strategies. During 1997, only a year after the new corporate communications department was formed, the firm's chairman participated in more than fifty  interviews with influential media, resulting in major feature articles in *The New York Times, The Washington Post, Financial Times, Business Week,* and *USA Today,* and numerous television appearances on CNN, CNBC, and PBS.

At the same time, we set a goal to build the company's role as a thought leader. In an environment where consumers of information want more than information, the chance to be perceived as a thought-leading firm that can provide advice, counsel, and insight is a great competitive advantage. The best way to do that is to make sure that in addition to talking about the firm and what it does, senior managers also speak about broader issues and trends. It is a "big picture" strategy. We contracted with The Gallup Organization to conduct a quarterly poll of investors to determine their impressions of the market and other factors that influenced the investing world. Called the Index of Investor Optimism, the study has become a favorite of the media, including *The Wall Street Journal,* and has ever been used by President Clinton's  economic advisors in their research. In effect, the study allowed PaineWebber to take ownership of the investor sentiment market.

We also sought issues-oriented platforms in which our senior executives could participate as thought leaders and talk about things other than the day-to-day operations and results of the firm. The most visible was Marron's participation in a bipartisan commission on Social Security reform. It was an issue perfectly suited to his experience and generated a lot of excellent media coverage.

In addition, we began to take the wealth of talent and information within the firm and customize it for our investors. As a firm with a reputation for having one of the best investment research departments on Wall Street, PaineWebber was sitting on mountains of information that was not getting distributed to the new generation of investors. Among our department's most successful efforts was a series of publications, supported by seminars with high-level analysts and strategists, targeted at the growing market of women investors. Called "Beyond the Basics: Investment Strategies for Women," this award-winning initiative took existing material, repackaged it at relatively low cost, and opened up communication between the firm's professionals and a new group of investors hungry for information and attention. The effort was so successful, that similar strategies were developed to target other potentially underserved investor groups, such as seniors and minorities.

We also brought the stock analysts closer to the firm. Using the same relationship-building methods we had used with the media, we communicated with the buy-side and sell-side analysts who covered the company, as well as the ones we wanted to cover the company but didn't. One-on-one meetings, conference calls, presentations by our senior management at investment community forums, and inhouse presentations to analysts all helped build the profile of the firm with this important audience. So successful was this effort that at the firm's annual meeting with analysts, held in January to review the previous year's results, more than sixty influential analysts attended. Five years earlier, only a handful would have been interested.

To complete the circle, we developed a comprehensive program for communicating with the firm's employees. The components included a monthly magazine for all employees, regular town meetings for employees at headquarters and in the field, periodic distribution of important strategic information from senior management, and a more complete store of information on the corporate Web site so that all staff would have instant access to news being made by the company.

The results were constructive. PaineWebber may not be the biggest firm on Wall Street, but it is certainly among the best known. Its people, from senior executives to research analysts and strategists, are newsmakers, opinion leaders, personalities. I don't think it's a stretch to say that Donald Marron, through our media strategy, became probably the most visible Wall Street chief executive in the late 1990s. His visibility was not simply tied to the firm's operation. He was sought out on a regular basis to provide expert commentary on a broad range of topics and issues. And while it took a little time to build his profile as well as the firm's, the payoff became obvious. When the generation of new investors tuned in to CNN to see Lou Dobbs and "Moneyline" on the night of Robert Rubin's resignation, the expert they saw was PaineWebber's chairman.

## Summary of Trends

▶ *The environment on Wall Street changed overnight, pushing brokerage firms from being shy violets to media darlings—from sleepy investment banks to consumer businesses.* Most were unprepared.

▶ *The dynamics that changed the game started with the rise of the individual investor.* Faced with new responsibility for their financial future, this group saw investing as a necessity, not a game for the idle rich.

▶ *Few of these new investors are sophisticated.* They are impressionable. The bull market of the 1990s has generated unhealthy enthusiasm and a feeling of invincibility. Their expectations are too high.

▶ *Consolidation in the industry has further confused investors.* There are few recognizable brand names. People are not sure whom to trust.

▶ *Money is among the most personal and emotional of all issues.* Businesses that manage people's money must take that factor into account. It is a strong determining factor in individual investors's motivations and behavior.

▶ *The media caught on quickly to the new demands of the individual investors.* They also understood that the dynamics of the situation—novices playing a high-stakes game—were pretty sexy. And they started looking to the Wall Street firms to see what they were doing to help these new investors understand the business.

## Lessons for Companies

▶ *Use the Wall Street lessons for guidance, especially if you are a new public company.* The environment has changed for your company, too, in that there are new audiences that want new information in new ways.

▶ *Don't be reactive.* Don't sit back. Make news. Establish a communications or public relations department soon. If you can, do it in-house. If not, start with an agency. It will not cost a lot, but it is essential.

▶ *Be consistent and professional in all your dealings with audiences, even in crises.* Speak with a single voice— even if there are several people speaking on your company's behalf, you must deliver a unified message.

▶ *Develop messages that are tied directly to your business strategy.* Remember, consumers and the media want to be educated about what you do and why. They don't simply want to know that you exist.

▶ *Develop relationships with the media outside the heat of battle.* Don't let day-to-day issues or a crisis be your only point of contact with reporters. Use the relationship-building process to learn their agendas, too.

▶ *Find ways to establish your company and your senior executives as thought leaders and opinion leaders.* Look for opportunities to have them speak about topics that aren't specific to your firm. This will enhance the reputation of your company and its products and services.

# CHAPTER 8

# Who's Out There?

## The Media's Audiences Are Your Customers

In the mid-1990s, a major Fortune 500 company decided to revamp its public relations activities because its reputation was less than zero. For the previous several years, it had been on a terrible reputational run with class action lawsuits, big payouts to customers, products that failed, and a series of other negative events that had tarnished the brand, which was well known and had been well respected. Bad publicity had forced the company into a bunker mentality. Its senior managers had stopped talking to everyone, both inside and outside the company. Relationships with the media and the investment community that followed the company were frayed or nonexistent. Employees wondered what the leadership was thinking, and more important, what it was going to do. No one inside or outside the company had any idea what the company's strategy was or how it planned to rebuild itself in the wake of the damage.

Making matters worse, the company was among a host of firms that were considered prime targets for takeover at a time when consolidation was making weekly headlines. Most of its competitors had declared some sort of strategy—or their consistent public profiles gave people a pretty good idea whether they were interested in being acquired. But the company in question was completely silent. Without a clearly articulated strategy, the

125

world could only speculate about what its management was thinking and what, eventually, it might do.

The company will remain nameless because the public relations work my firm performed for the senior management was prepared on a confidential basis. But the lessons learned from this experience are valuable. In fact, the results of the public relations project surprised the senior management in many ways. They had no idea the company was so disliked or misunderstood. They thought they had been doing a pretty good job of communicating, despite the bad press. It was a clear case of the senior management not being tuned in to its key audiences. The gap between them was what was stalling the company's attempt to rebuild its reputation.

## Gauging How People Feel About the Company

The most telling information came from the first stage of our project to revamp the firm's image. Public relations experts conducted a communications audit. This is market and customer research that gauges how people think and feel about a company. It consists of confidential telephone calls and face-to-face interviews with members of each influential audience to determine their perceptions of the company. What does the company do well? What does it do poorly? This audit focused on customers, employees, financial analysts, and members of the media who covered the company. There was one other audience that wound up offering a wealth of valuable information—senior management itself.

There is nothing quite so enlightening than having a mirror held up to yourself, and this audit did just that for the company in question. The survey revealed that customers of the company were worried. They feared that the company's problems of previous years were symptoms of a systemic problem, not isolated incidents. They also worried about merger or acquisition-related problems: What would happen in a transition? Would they keep the same sales representatives? Would the level of service suffer?

Employees were worried about their jobs. They feared that the firm's troubles had brought the company to its knees financially, and that the reason there had been no communication was that it was in danger of going under or being sold. Morale was low, and the rate of employee turnover was rising above industry averages.

Shareholders were worried about their investments. Not only was the company reeling from its problems, it had not developed a forward-looking strategy that would have given investors optimism about its ability to recover and rebuild its prosperity. The stock price lagged behind competitor's share prices.

Members of the media, of course, were livid. The company was unresponsive, they said, which, for a public company, was considered irresponsible. Reporters thought the company's public relations people were useless because they did not have access to the senior management. The public relations people were in a Catch-22 situation. Because they did not have access to senior management, they could not give reporters information about what the company was doing. The frustration on all sides was palpable.

The most startling feedback was from senior management itself. Managers were engaged in a bloody battle of blaming each other for the problems that had occurred. There was almost no effort to look ahead, to find solutions, to let bygones be bygones. Senior management was frozen, unable to move forward. And all the company's key audiences were in the dark. Worse, they were talking to each other about what they thought was going on at the company. The media talked to the analysts, customers, and employees. They all talked back to the media. But it was an exercise in speculation. Without any official word from the company, what else were they to do?

The lesson here is that you don't wait to find out what your key audiences think of you until it is too late. A crisis situation is not the time to try to build goodwill. You must always make sure you have some in the bank. Just because you are not saying anything doesn't mean that no one is saying anything about you.

And in this new media environment, where the flow of information is wide open, all your key audiences talk to each other, especially if they are not getting the kind of information and guidance they need from you.

James Taylor, coauthor of *The 500-Year Delta: What Happens After What Comes Next* and former Gateway 2000 marketing executive, said in an interview with *Fast Company* magazine (January 1997), that "[b]uilding a brand is about consistency. Every company, once it assumes a brand identity, has to live with the moral consequences of that identity. A brand is a promise, and you have to keep your promises. There's no difference between what we sell and who we are."

If you are small company that has just gone public, understanding what all your audiences think of you should be your first step in developing a communications program. Up until this point in the life of your company, you have probably only worried about one audience: your customers. As long as they are buying your products, life is good. You may also pay attention to your suppliers, but since you pay them to serve you, you are probably less concerned about their loyalty. Now that you have entered the world of publicly traded companies, however, the rules are different. You have to act like a public company, which means determining your most important audiences, finding out what they want to know about your company, and learning how they like to receive information. It is worth noting that a lot of very smart companies forget that last point. They spend lots of money on consumer and market research, develop extremely concise and strategic corporate messages, then distribute them through channels that reach only a small percentage of their key audiences. Remember, you can write the sweetest song in the world, but if no one listens to the radio, only a few people will hear it.

## Communicating Change Initiatives Internally

This point is worth an illustration. As a consultant, I was working with a major consumer company that had a very elaborate public relations machine that was adept at distributing the company's messages far and wide to several important audiences. But in the early 1990s, they came to my firm with a problem. They were trying to implement several cultural change initiatives, including some that would mean layoffs or early retirement packages for some workers. They were eager to manage the process properly and keep their employees up to speed because they were well aware that if their workforce read about the changes first in the media, there would hell to pay. Indeed, an important lesson is to make sure your employees hear from you first about any news the company is making, especially bad news. Nothing damages employee morale more than learning in the morning paper that their best friends have been laid off, and they might be next. Complicating the matter for this company was the fact that it had far-flung operations—plants, distribution centers, customer service centers, telemarketing operations, retail operations, and overseas distribution outlets.

Our first task on the project was to look at the initiatives, particularly the bad news. As part of the plan, there would be several thousand layoffs. This would indeed hurt morale and attract media attention. So the company was very smart to understand the need to take the high road and give its employees a heads-up. Our next task was to help the company decide what to say about these changes and who should say it. Our counsel was very direct. Do not try to sugar-coat the truth we advised. As hard as it is for people to hear that they and their friends will lose their jobs, there is nothing worse than some jargon-laden gobbledygook coming down from headquarters. We agreed that the messages should be direct and compassionate but not full of "spin."

We then decided that an announcement affecting so many people in the company should come from the chief executive. It would be appropriate for him or her to put the move into strategic terms. Besides, as small solace as it may be, people may feel better when the chief executive considers it important enough to handle the matter personally. Remember President Clinton. People would have been more forgiving if he had been truthful up front, even about a distasteful issue.

At our next step, we hit a roadblock. We had the information, we had the messages, and we had the man to deliver it. What channels of distribution should we use? The meeting room went silent. Then a meek voice from the corner chipped in, "Bulletin boards." The consultants at the table laughed. This giant, global consumer products company planned to make an announcement of this magnitude, affecting the livelihoods of many people, by posting a note on bulletin boards? We advised against it. But it was we consultants who didn't get it. Bulletin boards were the preferred—indeed the only consistent—channel through which employees in the field received information from corporate headquarters. Sure, from time to time, the regional and field managers would meet with their people to discuss issues and events, but formal communication with employees was accomplished by written memos pinned to cork boards in the cafeterias, smoking lounges, and other public areas in the company's operations.

We were dumbfounded. O.K., so this wasn't a technology company with a highly technology-literate workforce. But bulletin boards? All of a sudden, the company had a crisis within a crisis. Not only was this a completely inappropriate method of distributing news like this, but it could backfire in two ways. First, there was a good chance that a large percentage of the employee population might not look at their local bulletin boards the day the announcement was posted, in which case they would probably hear about the situation first from either a fellow employee or the media. Second, and potentially more damaging, the media might learn of the inadequacy of the company's internal systems and generate more negative publicity. I could picture the headlines now: "You're Fired. See Bulletin Board No. 4 by the Coffee Machine. How XYZ Told 6,000 Employees Goodbye."

We needed to figure out a way not only to avert a potential crisis but also to bolster the company's credibility in a very difficult situation. We recommended  an immediate meeting between the chief executive and all the regional and division managers to brief everyone on the issue and give out the marching orders. The process would unfold as follows: On the day of the announcement, each employee would receive at his or her home a letter from the chief executive officer explaining the situation and the rationale behind it. That would cover anyone who did not make it to work for whatever reason. At the same time, shortly before the public announcement, the divisional, regional, and facility managers would each hold meetings to announce the news to all their employees. The chief executive and other senior management members would take care of that task at headquarters. Following these meetings, a news release would be issued, and the chief executive would be available for media interviews.

## Getting the Message Out Effectively

The goal was to deliver the news in as personal a way as possible. Because the company was so big and so ill-equipped to handle this kind of communication, a teleconference was out of the question. The company did not know how to arrange such a thing, and the workforce was not used to receiving its information that way. Besides, a talking head on a television screen a thousand miles away does not have the same impact as a person, presumably one an employee recognizes and knows, delivering the news.

It was also important to get the news to all the people at the same time and before the media got it. That was only fair. In addition, by limiting the notice to employees on the day of the announcement, the risk of a leak was reduced. And herein lies a lesson that companies, even smart ones, often forget. Anything your company distributes internally should be considered a public document. Very often internal memos have ended up in reporters' hands or analysts' hands or customers' hands and generated news stories. Therefore, don't say anything in an internal memo that you would not say to the public. Even though an internal memo is addressed to an employee, that may not be its final destination. Finally, another important reason for informing employees ahead of the media is to prevent any surprised reaction interviews with the media that would reflect badly on your company.

As a follow-up to the strategy for the day of the announcement, we recommended that in the following weeks, the chief executive or other members of senior management visit as many of the facilities as they could to hold town meetings to discuss the firings. The meetings were important for two reasons. First, the personal appearance of a senior official would win points internally and externally for the senior management team. Second, it would boost morale with those employees who remained, an important point considering that they were probably feeling angry at the company for laying off friends and colleagues as well as uncertain and vulnerable about their own jobs. A senior official appearing in person to calm the waters would be an important element in restoring peace of mind to the workers and stability to the company's operations.

The strategy was implemented according to plan. The managers performed their duties admirably considering it was an extremely difficult task. No memos were posted on the bulletin boards. Were the employees angry? Some were, to be sure. There is absolutely no way to make bad news good, no matter how sincerely and professionally it is delivered. But the anger was not widespread, and many employees were surprised and impressed that the company's management had made the effort to become personally involved in the issue. The bulletin boards, it seemed, were considered to be a reflection of the fact that senior management didn't care. The way it was handled in this case was considered by most, inside and outside the company, to be a good job under trying circumstances.

There was one other recommendation we made to the company as part of this strategy: It should spend the money to build a workable internal communications network. It now has a comprehensive menu of options—an intranet with e-mail, Internet access for a large percentage of employees, a special employee section on the corporate Web site, a company magazine, and electronic bulletin boards for the people who work either in plants or other facilities where their jobs do not allow easy access to computers.

Considering that there are more audiences out there seeking information about you, companies must be more diverse in their delivery of media messages than ever before. The key is to understand not only who the different audiences are and what they want to know, but also how they like to receive information. The bulletin board story is only one example. Think about the way your customers may have changed their habits, particularly with the advent of technology. They may be shopping more online or by using direct mail. They may be using toll-free telephone numbers to place orders for merchandise and information. They may be shopping from catalogues, or they may still prefer going to the mall for certain purchases.

Think back to the late 1980s and early 1990s when the experts said the rise of the videocassette player and recorder and the mass marketing of videos would kill the motion picture industry. People would eventually stop going to movies, the video advocates said, because there would be no reason to spend $7, $8 or even $10 to go to a movie theater with a noisy bunch of people who spill drinks on the floor and munch popcorn in your ear. What better way to enjoy a movie than at home, in peace and quiet, at whatever time you liked for only $3.

## Customers Want More Choice, Not Less

The logic was taken to even greater extremes when pay-per-view video and video-on-demand technology appeared. At the time, I was a reporter for *The Miami Herald*, and one of the companies I covered was Blockbuster Entertainment Corp., then based in Fort Lauderdale and now based in Dallas. Its chief executive was Wayne Huizenga, a former Waste Management executive who went on to a number of other successful ventures, including ownership of several Florida sports teams. At the time, however, video was his business, and his company was the runaway leader. It was opening a store almost every day, and the revenue the company generated was more than enough to fund its expansion. Remarkably, a company with such fast growth had absolutely no debt. And despite the huge success of his company, Huizenga was a careful guy. He had not believed that the video market would kill the motion picture industry. Indeed, as someone who had become an expert at distribution channels, he figured video rentals would actually enhance the movie industry by providing a healthy after-market for movies, especially those that might not have been compelling enough on the big screen to attract a lot of viewers. And with the cost of movie production skyrocketing, Hollywood was looking for any way to extend the revenue-generating potential of its product. Video was a perfect vehicle.

Huizenga had the same opinion about pay-per-view and video-on-demand and their impact on the video rental business. These new channels would give viewers more options and provide Hollywood with yet another way to squeeze out profits. The investment community that followed Blockbuster was not convinced. Blockbuster's senior management suffered through endless conference calls and research reports projecting doom and gloom for the video rental industry by as early as 1995. Huizenga, a normally calm, down-to-earth fellow, took the criticism in stride, though he shook his head and said his critics didn't get it. But what made his blood boil was the fact that Blockbuster's stock was a favorite among short-sellers—investors who take positions betting a stock will fall. That really burned him, because it meant that at least some investors believed the analysts' forecasts of video-rental Armageddon.

Well, 1995 came and went, and Blockbuster is still around and doing well. People still enjoy renting movies, and pay-per-view and video-on-demand are still around, too. Cable television has grown to the point where home cable packages usually include a selection of several movie channels such as HBO, Starz, and The Movie Channel, among others. And the movie theaters are full, too. A lot of people still enjoy the excitement and experience of going out to the movies, of seeing a film on the big screen. Technology has helped. Better production quality, better projection and lighting equipment, and huge improvements in sound quality have made movie-going a great experience again. And while Wayne Huizenga is off doing other things now—and while he isn't the kind of guy to say he told you so—I'll say it for him. He told you so. The point is that in this environment, people want more choice, not less. Those who say the opposite have been proven wrong. Your company must understand that dynamic and offer all your audiences as many choices as they demand to get information about what you are doing.

The media are no different in this sense. A Generation X journalist may like to receive information about your company online, sweeping your corporate Web site and corresponding with you through e-mail. By contrast, a reporter for *Business Week* will probably want to spend time interviewing you, both in person and on the telephone. A television reporter has completely different needs. She may simply want eight or ten minutes with you on-camera for some quick sound bites. Or a television anchor may want you in the studio for a twenty-minute taping.

Investment analysts, too, have changing preferences, mostly influenced by the boom in technology. While research is highly competitive and proprietary, the fact-gathering process of analysts has been broadened and enhanced by e-mail and the Internet. Many companies now cater to this growing demand by posting earnings releases on their corporate Web sites before conference calls with analysts. The logic is that the analysts don't have to hunt down faxed copies of releases as the conference call is beginning. Eventually, certain companies plan to allow analysts to ask questions during the calls via e-mail. Some companies are already experimenting with technology that will allow them to broadcast such conference calls on their corporate Web sites in real-time, with the script of the call available on site at the same time. The beauty of such a set-up is that with password protection, companies can control the participants in the call. They can limit the calls to analysts who register with them. Participation will be by invitation only, but those who are invited get to see members of senior management, not just hear them. This, experts say, will be the way of the future for conference calls.

How does your company figure out who your audiences are, what information they need, and how they want to receive it? If you are an established company, you may think you have a pretty good idea. My suggestion is that you revisit the situation soon. Technology has changed the world so much so quickly that common practices a couple of months ago may be outdated today. If you are a company that is new to technology, it is imperative that you do this soon.

## Surveying Your Audience

The first step is to conduct a survey—or communications audit. It will cost a few dollars but will be well worth the money to learn who is saying what about your company and why. It will also answer these questions:

▶ What information do your audiences want most?

▶ How do they want to get the information?

▶ How is your company serving their needs now?

▶ What does your company do well? What needs improvement?

While the media and customers are important, don't forget your internal audience, namely your employees, including all levels of management. Remember the examples highlighted here. They are not only consumers of information but also ambassadors for the company with all outside audiences. Serving their needs can have a positive ripple effect. Ignoring them can have an equally negative effect. Your key audiences will be either misinformed or not informed at all. The resulting vacuum will be filled with speculation.

There's another important reason that the audit is not simply an exercise for young companies that may not have developed a profile. Many mature companies have gone through restructuring. Some have merged, some have acquired another company, and some have been acquired. All companies in these situations can benefit from this exercise. The reason: A communications audit is a baseline from which all communications, inside and outside the company, can be developed. If you have recently undergone significant changes in your organization, you are basically a new company again. You need to reconnect with your audiences. You need to know what these audiences—old and new—are saying about you, good and bad, inside and out. You need a new place to start, and you need to know the new set of issues on which you must build your new strategy. Don't guess about what's important to the audiences that are most important to you.

## Conducting an Audit

The beauty of an audit is that it is conducted anonymously, so the respondents don't know your company is asking for their opinions. In addition, if the respondents know that they are being quoted anonymously, they are more likely not to hold back. This is particularly important when taking the pulse of the audience inside your company. Finally, the anonymity factor will be particularly useful when canvassing senior management. These are the people who often have the strongest opinions but the most to lose by airing them, especially if they are negative.

There are a few rules to follow when commissioning an audit. The main rule is to have the project completed properly and with input from as many sources as possible. There is the danger that if such a project is done only halfway, the information obtained from it may lead to incorrect conclusions. And incorrect conclusions can lead to flawed strategy. That, in turn, can create problems that didn't exist before or that make a bad situation even worse. Follow these guidelines:

> ▶ *Use an outside firm.* Most public relations firms are skilled at conducting such studies. Ideally, former jour-

nalists should be the ones conducting the interviews. It is important to have someone who knows how to extract information from people. Typically, these audits are conducted using a questionnaire from which the interviewer reads. If not done well, the respondent will answer only the questions and give no more information. A skilled interviewer knows how to follow up, how to lead an interview and explore issues more deeply. When checking out a possible firm to conduct the survey, ask whom they will use as the interviewer and what his or her qualifications are. Work with the interviewer to develop the questions, and give him or her some guidance—or best guesses—on where certain issues might lead. The more information the interviewer has beforehand, the more information he or she is likely to come away with.

In addition, you need to hire an outside firm so the survey seems impartial to the people who participate in it. An outside firm is more likely to elicit more genuine responses from respondents. If an inhouse staff member conducts the audit, the credibility will be tainted for those inside and outside the company. Respondents will be less likely to be forthcoming and will try to "spin" their answers, thinking that eventually their identities will be revealed as the sources of critical comments. They will not tell all to an internal person, and that will render ineffective the survey and the strategy that springs from it.

▶ *Maintain and ensure anonymity for everyone involved.* This is very important. As a manager, you must make sure that your company's name is not identified as the one conducting the survey. Survey language can be used to get around this. For example, a questioner can say he or she is doing some market research on the shoe industry and wants perceptions about the following three companies. Yours is one of them, but it is not singled out. It is a good idea for you to take the survey to determine if the questions contain some language or terminology that might identify your company.

▶ *Ask the firm doing the survey to record direct quotes from the people it interviews.* There is nothing so powerful in driving home the message of an audit than recording and reporting direct quotes. If a senior manager sees that those who report directly to him consider him "an overbearing know-it-all who wouldn't know empowerment if it kicked him in the rear end," he is more likely to pay attention than if he reads a paraphrase that says "middle management expressed concerns in a few areas regarding its responsibility and authority."

Again, think of the power of the written word. You can sit in meetings all day long and talk about an idea or a concept until you're blue in the face and not get the response you want. But put it down on paper—make it real, make it tangible—and people pay attention. The same is true in the case of audit reporting. Printed comments, especially if they are critical, gets people's attention. They can't pretend they didn't hear them. They can't dismiss them as easily as they might like. Truth may hurt, but in the end, it is an effective vehicle of change.

▶ *Have the PR firm interview all audiences.* Don't just concentrate on a few. Remember, all of your key audiences—customers, shareholders, employees, the media, analysts and others—are now all talking to each other, or at least exchanging information with each other. So it is important to know the messages that are spread through the grapevine. In particular, don't ignore your internal audiences. Top-to-bottom perceptions are important. Again, concentrate on getting senior managers to participate. They may be reluctant, but press them. Strange as it may seem, senior managers, who are supposed to be the key communicators of information about the company, often don't consider it important to get information from each other.

▶ *Don't be alarmed if your audit turns up some of the same results that were delivered to the financial services company highlighted at the beginning of this chapter.* Remember, the audit surprised everyone at the company, particularly the senior management. Your management, too, may think it is doing a pretty good job of talking to everyone, but the audit may tell you they aren't. It may also tell you that your senior managers aren't even doing a good job of talking to each other.

▶ *If you're the chief executive officer, be prepared to take some criticism.* Remember, you asked for it. The chief executive of that Fortune 500 company was considered aloof, even secretive. The senior managers felt they had little input into the strategic direction of the company and, in fact, were being given small, task-focused slices of the corporate pie. How do you think you will be perceived? Do you have a good idea about whether your senior managers feel empowered?

▶ *Pay close attention to the way your employees respond.* If the study is done properly and carefully, you will probably learn more about your company from these respondents than anyone else. For example, the rank and file of a struggling financial services company had a complete indifference to the company. When asked whether they liked working for the company, most shrugged. Few were excited but some thought it was a bad place to work. How do your employees feel about working for you? Are they proud of your company and the products and services it produces? Do they believe in the company and its senior management? What do they tell their friends, neighbors and acquaintances—all of them, perhaps, potential customers of your company?

To no one's surprise, in the case of the financial services company, the external audiences had very bad things to say about it. The media thought the public relations group was useless, mainly because they did not have sufficient access to senior management, which had no credibility whatsoever. Do the media feel the same way about your company? Do they have enough access to good information? Can you do better? Should you do better? What impact is the media's view of you having on your other key audiences?

Customers of the company in question, too, had difficulty attaching to the brand name any significant characteristics that supported their decision to use the company's products and services—or to consider it as an investment. There was nothing, they said, that distinguished the company from its competitors. Therefore, there was no compelling reason for customers to choose the company. Several customers, when pressed, actually felt embarrassed that they were doing business with the company and could not identify any good reasons for their decision. Do your customers feel the same way about you? In their eyes, what do you stand for? What makes you different from and better than your competitors? Do your customers feel good not only about your products and services but also about their experience in dealing with your company? Would they recommend you to a friend?

Remember, that in this environment of increasing choice, your company must make a compelling case to its key audiences. They must have a clear idea of why they do business with you or work for you. They must be certain that the products and services they buy from you are of value and that they are dealing with a company that makes them feel good about their choice.

## Summary of Trends

► *The audiences of most companies are more diverse than ever before.* They want to know more and have more choices in the way they get information about companies.

► *The environment is one where the trend is toward more choice, not less.* Distribution channels are become more numerous. Consumers, more adept at managing technology, are demanding a variety of distribution channels and customized information on channel. In addition, choices change more frequently as new technology appears.

► *New public companies are at risk because they are not accustomed to understanding and catering to so many diverse audiences in an environment of increasing choice.*

► *Mature companies are not immune to the challenges.* With technology, audiences' preferences can change overnight. What appealed to a key audience a few months ago may be obsolete by now.

► *Companies that have gone through significant changes are in the same position as new companies.* They don't know their audiences, and their audiences don't know them.

## Lessons for Companies

► *Don't be complacent.* Don't guess at what information your audiences want and how they want to get it. Find out.

▶ *Conduct a communications audit of all your audiences, including internal ones, especially senior management.* Be tough on yourself. Ask tough questions. Be thorough.

▶ *Use an independent service to conduct the audit.* Impartiality will improve the response rate and the amount of valuable information you retrieve.

▶ *Have a former journalist or other professional interviewer conduct the audit if possible.* Work with the interviewer to draft the questions and alert him or her to the issues you need to know more about.

▶ *Maintain and ensure anonymity for all involved.* This will improve the response rate and the value of the information. Respondents will be more forthcoming, more willing to speak their minds.

▶ *If you are the chief executive, prepare yourself for criticism.* Truth may hurt, but it is valuable in building a company that serves all your key audiences.

▶ *Use the results of the audit as a baseline for all your future communications.* Test ideas against it. It will provide a valuable litmus test for your strategy.

▶ *Update the audit regularly.* With preferences and choices changing quickly, be sure you are not making decisions based on out-of-date information, even if it is only a few months old.

# CHAPTER 9

# The Kid in the Candy Store
## Overcoming the Temptations of Plenty

I n the spring of 1991, I was the assistant business editor of *The Miami Herald* and was assigned to spend a day with Donald Trump. "The Donald" was coming to Miami as a guest of the *Herald's* publisher, David Lawrence, to be the keynote speaker at an annual luncheon held to honor the paper's Company of the Year candidates. The award was a public relations gesture, not uncommon in markets the size of Miami. The business community seemed to like it, and it kept relations good between the paper and its major advertisers. While it was usually the same crop of businesses selected as finalists each year, the paper covered the event as if it were a real news story and played it up prominently, both before the fact and afterward, in the next day's edition. As successful as the event was, it never quite played to a full house. There were usually a few empty seats at a few tables, presumably left vacant by those who had found a better offer than stale bread sticks and rubber chicken. The Donald was about to change all that.

In the months leading up to his appearance at the *Herald* lunch, Trump had made a quite a splash in South Florida, having bought two derelict waterfront apartment buildings in the midst of the biggest regional real estate recession in years and turned them into luxury condominiums. He also purchased Mar-a-Lago, the waterfront Palm Beach estate formerly owned by the Post cereal

family. And while he had frightened the Palm Beach zoning commission with a threat to turn the showpiece property into a condo-
minium development or a club, he made even more outrageous
demands of the city that annoyed many of the denizens of the tony
enclave. The most memorable move was his petition to have the
flight paths changed at Palm Beach International Airport. The reason: One of the runways accommodated low-flying aircraft that
took off or landed right over his house. The noise and vibration
were driving him nuts. So Trump was a local story at the time.

In the meantime, he had some issues in his life up north to deal
with. He was still embroiled with the bankers who had financed his
struggling real estate and casino empires in New York and Atlantic
City. The media had reported he was broke and washed up. Yet he
continued to negotiate with the banks as if he had the upper hand.
Remarkably, and to most everyone's surprise but his own, he struck
a deal with the banks and remained in business.

But the Florida purchases, his publicity stunts, and the
intriguing high-stakes drama surrounding his casinos were not the
real reason that tickets to the *Herald* luncheon featuring Donald
Trump sold out. Trump was involved in not only a high-profile
divorce from his wife, Ivana, but also in a torrid and very public
love affair with a young actress named Marla Maples. His personal
life was front-page news almost every day in New York, and was
regularly covered by television and radio stations. The images were
memorable. An incensed Ivana would appear on camera, trashing
her soon-to-be ex-husband for stiffing her with an unfair prenup-
tial agreement that would leave her with a paltry post-divorce settlement of only a few million dollars. Trump and Maples would
appear in separate footage, either coming or going from some
glitzy high-profile gathering in Manhattan, all smiles and kisses. It
had all the elements of a soap opera worthy of network television:
wealth, power, love, scorn, betrayal, and beauty.

So when Trump's 727, its fuselage emblazoned with huge
letters that spelled his name, landed that April morning at Miami
International Airport, the air was electric with anticipation. As the
reporter assigned to shadow him for the day, I and a couple of

senior executives from the newspaper and its parent company, Knight-Ridder, were waiting for him in a limousine.

He was personable and chatty, a strange mix of bravado and childlike wonder at all that was going on around him. As we drove through the streets of Miami, he would point out properties and buildings and ask us whether they were for sale. "I could do a lot with that place," he would mutter. At one point, he engaged one of the *Herald* executives in a long discussion about the possibility of casino gambling being approved in Florida. He was disappointed to learn that there was limited support for the concept. "Boy," he said, peering out the car window as if he were a little boy seeing big buildings for the first time, "wouldn't it be great to gamble and go to the beach here."

But the real excitement occurred when the car stopped at the hotel where the luncheon was being held. Outside, a mob of reporters was waiting. There were maybe a hundred of them— camera crews, print reporters with notebooks, radio reporters with tape recorders and microphones poised to thrust them into Trump's face the minute he arrived. Several reporters held copies of that morning's New York tabloids, the *Daily News* and the *Post*, both of which featured full, front-page photos of Trump with Marla Maples and accompanying shots of an angry Ivana.

Trump hesitated. He sat for a moment, looking out at the throng that was pushing against the car and peering in to see what was going on. At first, I thought he was concerned. Or maybe he was just exhausted at the prospect of pushing his way through yet another herd of frantic reporters asking probing questions about his love life. But I was wrong. After another moment or two, he turned to look at us and with a smile said, "Damn good for business, isn't it?" Chuckling, he declared "Showtime!" and burst out of the car into the mob.

## Is All Publicity Good Publicity?

Trump had become adept at using the media as a tool. Or so he thought. All this publicity, no matter what it was about, kept his name and face in the papers. It didn't matter that the biggest part of it involved a scandalous affair and divorce. It was clear that in his mind, any and all publicity was good publicity. He believed the saying, "It's when people stop talking about you that it's time to worry."

True, some media mock him and portray him as something less than the stylish playboy-mogul he paints himself to be. It is clear that Trump either doesn't see it that way or he doesn't care. And he has the luxury of deep pockets to ignore his detractors. But his belief that the circus atmosphere that surrounds his personal life is good for business raise interesting points of discussion. How much exposure is too much? At what point does the media and those who use the media begin to see through his game? And at what point does the publicity become a liability to the credibility of the man and his business alike?

## Overexposure Can Be Damaging

Here's another example that raises similar questions. When Al Dunlap took over Sunbeam, he had already become a master at playing the media. In fact, the media seized hungrily on his nickname, "Chainsaw Al," which referred to the swift, noisy, and messy ways he gutted the failing companies he was hired to rescue. He was a master of laying off thousands of employees in the name of efficiency. He was considered to be ruthless in his approach to dismissing senior managers who did not see the world the way he saw it. Indeed, in the wake of the "go-go 1980s," when companies got fat and happy, Dunlap's "my way or the highway" approach to corporate turnarounds made him something of a media darling.

Indeed, in the early to mid-1990s, it was virtually impossible to pick up a newspaper or magazine or turn on the television without seeing Dunlap spinning his corporate restructuring wisdom following some huge layoff of his own doing. He no longer talked only about the companies with which he was involved. When asked, which was often, he would offer his expert opinion on almost any company out there, making bold suggestions about what he might do if he were in charge. He would deliver his opinions in a gruff, no-nonsense tone, with inflections that suggested he could figure out why companies weren't run this way all the time. To say that Chainsaw and his brand of corporate restructuring were ubiquitous is perhaps an overstatement, but only slightly.

But unlike Trump, it became clear that Dunlap began to believe his own hype. He considered the media to be his friend, his ally, a willing participant in his rise to stardom. And why wouldn't he? In a business world filled with stuffed shirts or reclusive technology nerds, Dunlap was a real live rootin' tootin' cowboy. He shot from the hip and wasn't afraid to be outrageous. He even looked the part, wearing flashy suits with wide stripes. He was a novelty act, to be sure, but at the time he had success to back up his stardom. He had done things the best managers in the world had not done—taken companies that had one foot in the grave and made them successes. The fact that he had used methods that were far from kind and gentle was secondary—they worked.

His comeuppance came when irregularities started showing up in Sunbeam's books. Sales of barbecue grills were recorded in December, for example, and electric blankets were booked as sales in mid-summer. This fiddling with the books, whether he was aware of it or not, became his undoing. The media that had once been his friend grew fangs. To spin himself out of trouble, he hired a major New York public relations agency. But he was already overexposed. His efforts to garner favor again could not overcome the fact that his credibility as a business person had been damaged. Indeed, the accounting irregularities aroused the suspicion that all of his other so-called miracle corporate turnarounds might not have been clean plays. Maybe he had used smoke and mirrors after all. Dunlap tried one last time to use the media, to spin himself out of trouble, but his old friends, the reporters, didn't love him anymore. And the media are unforgiving when it comes to their roles as defenders of the truth, whether you believe them or not.

## When Any Publicity Is Bad Publicity

Here's another example of thinking the media can solve problems: In 1995 a high-profile client was embroiled in a global scandal that had caught the attention of the U.S. government. So deep was his involvement, investigators said, that he faced indictment on a number of fraud and espionage charges.

When he called me and a couple of colleagues into his office, which offered a spectacular floor-to-ceiling view of the East River in Manhattan, his idea was to tell his side of the story to *The Washington Post*. He had a reporter friend there, he said, who would believe everything he said. He had a good story to tell, he said, with airtight evidence that he was not to blame for the charges leveled against him. If he could only get the reporter to listen, his story would blow holes in the government's case and keep him out of jail. Fists clenched and banging on the desk, this usually composed and soft-spoken man let emotion drive his decision-making. A war hero and son of a war hero, he could not understand why his country had turned against him, he insisted. "This is personal," he said. "It's no longer business."

But it was our business to keep him from making a bad situation worse, which we believed he would do if he went to *The Washington Post*, reporter friend or no reporter friend. We explained to him that a good reporter, especially at a newspaper like the *Post*, would have to check out the other side of the story, too, and was obliged by the ethical restraints of the news business to tell both sides. Our sense was that his story, while possibly true, was built upon hearsay and other circumstantial facts that, when laid against the investigators' findings, would look weak. The damage of going public with such a weak case, we believed, would make matters worse, not better. Not only would he go to jail, he would make a fool of himself by offering up a preposterous story in his own defense.

We had several meetings during the next few weeks, all covering the same ground and all ending with him wanting to go to the *Post* and our advising against it. At that point, we decided to invoke an oft-used but usually poorly executed public relations tool called a best-case/worst case scenario which show a client a close approximation of what his story would look like if told to the media.

As a former national business journalist, I was selected to produce a mock-up of a *Washington Post* article based on this client's story. I researched the issue as if I were back wearing my reporter's hat. I searched archives and clipping services for articles that had been written about it. I obtained public documents that outlined the government's case and spoke with as many people involved in the case as I could without jeopardizing the confidentiality of the client's identity. From this, I wrote a feature-length article, mocked up in newspaper style with a headline and photographs. For all intents and purposes, it was the real thing in that I had once done this for a living. And it was clearly damaging to the client. When stacked up, in black and white, his story was even weaker than we had anticipated. His evidence was flimsy, his sources weak, his recollection of events spotty. As we said, whether his story was true or not ceased to be the issue. The issue was that if he told his story to a reporter at a respected and responsible newspaper like the *Washington Post*, he would be crucified.

When we arrived at the client's office for a follow-up meeting to present the article, we were confident that what we had produced would be effective. But we were worried that the emotional unsteadiness of the client might cause him to make a mistake. We presented the client and his lawyers with copies of the article, and the room fell silent. The client read it once, put it down on the table in front of him for a moment, and said, "Jesus." Then he picked it up and read it again. Finishing the article the second time, he said, "You're right." Then he got up and walked out of the office. That was the last time I saw him until the trial, which was swift and not in his favor.

There are a number of lessons here. But most important is that with the abundance of media out there, particularly with the growth of technology, there's a great temptation to get as much of it as you can. The media may have their faults, and there may be a talent deficit out there, but make no mistake. Reporters are not dumb. And most of them have become pretty adept at figuring out who the hucksters are. Unless you see yourself like Donald Trump, for whom any and all exposure apparently is O.K., then be careful. Managing your media exposure looks easy, but that's not true.

First, overexposure is just as bad as not enough exposure. Second, the media is not your friend. If you're flying high in business and things are going well, you may think the media love you. Be careful. You are simply a good story. You will be just as good a story—maybe better—when times turn tough. You will get just as much attention, maybe more. Ask Al Dunlap. And don't make the mistake of fighting your battles in the media. Reporters are bound by responsibility to tell both sides of a story. If the other side has a better, stronger story than yours, you have a problem. Telling it rarely fixes anything, and often it makes a bad situation even worse.

## Disinformation Overload

The explosion in the variety of business news outlets presents companies and their people with a tempting smorgasbord. The media's need to fill space has created an enormous demand for content. Journalists are hungry to talk to anyone they can get their hands on. They are becoming less and less picky about the qualifications of the sources they choose to use. That's a problem for a credible source because if it is lumped in with all the others, it will be considered no better than the worst.

One of the first rules in public relations, and media relations in particular, is to make sure that not only what you say is credible, but where you say it is credible as well. The medium can have an impact on the message. A suspect media outlet will, by virtue of its own weaknesses, dilute the power of your messages. In contrast, a good media outlet can improve your lot, but most good media outlets don't have to go picking through the bottom of the barrel for sources.

Still, for many media outlets, it is obvious that the quality of the context and sourcing of stories is of secondary concern. As long as there is someone talking, it is considered useful information. Think back again to the Monica Lewinsky scandal in the Clinton White House. When the reporters ran out of facts to report and qualified experts to discuss their opinions, they began interviewing other reporters. Anything to fill time and space and keep the ball rolling. The downside, of course, is that such situations cause information overload—or rather disinformation overload. There is more chatter, but less substance. More sizzle, less steak. And though the buzz is louder, the quality is lower. At some point, even the hungriest media junkies will tune out. That means your message will get lost, or worse, jumbled.

The keys for companies to remember in this media environment are pretty simple. You must resist the temptation to be everywhere all the time. It is not a good strategy. But it's easy to let your eyes get bigger than your stomach when the media feast is so plentiful. Selectivity is crucial to building a proper media profile. Even as a young company, eager to get media exposure any way you can, be choosy. Put your efforts into building relationships with good reporters and respectable media outlets. Don't chase the quick hits. You would rather have one decent story in *The Wall Street Journal* or an influential trade magazine than a whole stack of clips from outlets considered to be lean on credibility or, even worse, not being chosen by your key audiences as important sources of information.

## Selecting Your Media Contacts

How do you determine which media outlets and journalists are credible? If your company has a media list, rework it with a more critical eye. If you don't have one, hire someone to put one together. It isn't brain surgery, but it requires a knowledge of the media and the company and its strategy. It doesn't have to be a long list. Prioritize. Start with your own preferences. As the business head, you have better instincts than you think. Which media do you trust? Which do your colleagues and customers trust? Don't be afraid to ask.

Like any list of important contacts, it needs regular upkeep. Even the best companies fall short on list maintenance. It is the key to ensuring that your messages get directly into the hands of the journalists who are most interested in them and who will use them. Misdirected information will simply be discarded. This is particularly important in the online environment, which is growing in influence but changing so quickly. New online news services appear almost daily, and reporters move freely from place to place. With the media explosion, the turnover of reporters is fast and furious, and in many cases you never know where reporters will turn up next.

Again, find out how your media contacts like to receive their information. Don't fax them releases if they prefer e-mail attachments. Don't pitch story ideas to them by telephone if they prefer to get them via e-mail. How do you find out all this stuff? A decent public relations agency can help, but you can also begin by subscribing to a couple of media journals. The best are TJFR and the Bulldog Reporters, which are basically cheat sheets for public relations executives. They regularly document the movement of reporters and editors between outlets and often give listings of entire business departments at influential outlets that include descriptions of each reporter's and editor's responsibilities and their phone, fax, and e-mail addresses. One of the most useful features of these lists is the notations about how the reporters prefer to get information. Increasingly, they want it via e-mail. But no matter what the method, such a tool will help you get your message directly to the people who matter most.

When putting together the key messages you plan to distribute, be focused. Resist the temptation to participate in media interviews on issues that are irrelevant to your business or do not fit your strategy. They are a waste of time and a threat to your credibility. Besides, there will be other opportunities soon, so have a little patience. I have worked with chief executives of several small companies who are so eager to get notices that they will jump at any opportunity, even if it has nothing to do with what they do. One client, who runs a consulting firm in Florida, once asked our firm to find issues in the media about which he could comment, whether the issues were related to his company's core strengths or not. It was a peculiar way of drumming up business, and it was deceitful. We recommended against it. In the end, the client managed to bluff his way onto television as an expert consultant on telecommunications mergers and acquisitions. For the first half of the interview, he sounded pretty believable. He talked about issues, the problems of integration, and the challenges of merging two cultures. Then came the "gotcha". The interviewer asked the consultant to talk about some of the telecom mergers and acquisitions on which he had worked and how he had solved the problems and issues he had raised. The client was stunned. He looked into the camera and said nothing. Of course, he had never been involved with one of these deals in his life. Everything he knew he had read in the newspapers or in some management consultant textbook. The interviewer interjected, "You know, maybe just a couple of real-life examples so our viewers can get a sense of how this stuff really works." The jig was up. The consultant squirmed a little in his chair and coughed. "Well," he began, "I'm not really at liberty to discuss the actual work I've done for clients because of confidentiality agreements, but I can tell you that some of the stuff we worked on was pretty interesting." He was dead in the water. Totally exposed. Credibility challenged. The interviewer immediately cut off the questioning and went to a commercial. It was the last time I ever saw the consultant quoted in the media. He was not asked back.

The problem is that many public relations people aren't at all selective. In this case, they would have seen only the opportunity to get their client on TV rather than the quality of his appearance. And I bet more than half of them would not have seen the downside of this consultant participating in a charade. Either they simply don't understand that media for media's sake is not a good idea, or they are so driven to generate billable hours that they simply don't care.

## Not All Media Opportunities Are Appropriate

On this point, let me give you an example. When I first left the world of journalism for public relations, my value, I was told, was that I understood where the media was coming from. I understood their agenda. I was a valuable sounding board for a company's message. If it didn't make sense to me, or it didn't sound sincere, or the numbers didn't add up, I gave it the thumbs down. At the time, I was the best devil's advocate around. I was skeptical, I was cynical, I was allergic to spin. And that angered certain account managers whose job it was to give clients what they wanted. The problem was that what the clients wanted and what the media wanted were not always the same. Our job was to bring them closer together so that we could still get the client's story out but in a way that was credible and digestible for the media. That's why clients paid us $200 to $300 an hour—to translate their speak into media speak. But from time to time, an over-eager account manager would become frustrated with me and other former journalists who refused to give in if we truly believed that a client's message would not fly. Because if we gave the green light to such a message, it would be our fault, not the account manager's or the client's. We were the experts. We made the calls.

I remember one such account manager, a relatively senior guy, whose client, a mid-level manager for the acquiring company in a pending merger, was eager to speak to the media about his view of the deal. We in the media group agreed that the client was certainly personable and knew his stuff, but he was clearly the wrong guy. Why on earth would a mid-level manager in a big company be speaking about a deal instead of the senior management? We advised the account manager that this was a bad idea because first, his client was an inappropriate spokesperson who would not be perceived by the media to have the information they needed about the deal, and second, he could get himself in a lot of trouble with the top brass if quotes from him started appearing in articles without authorization. "But," the account manager said at the height of his frustration, "*The New*

*York Times* would love to talk to this guy." Our response: "*The New York Times* doesn't *need* to talk to this guy. It can go right to the top. When *The New York Times* calls, senior executives pick up the phone." The account manager stormed out of the meeting, then stuck his head back in for a parting shot. "You know," he said, red-faced with frustration, "you media guys are too negative."

When choosing a public relations counselor, be sure there is someone on your account team who knows how the media thinks and works. Everything you want to say should be run by them. And if your account manager simply becomes a yes man—if his counsel and criticism are not constructive—beware. The role of a counselor is to be straight up with a client, to warn him or her when an idea or a plan isn't a good one. Naysaying, if done constructively, is a good thing—it could save you from costly mistakes.

More important, when looking at media opportunities, give each one the acid test—what's in it for you and your company? If the benefits are not clear or are outweighed by the potential downside, pass. There will be other opportunities that fit your agenda more closely.

## Deciding Who Speaks for Your Company

And if you don't have a media policy governing who can talk to reporters, put one in place now. This is not a police action. It is important for the management of your messages. Designate a central point person to whom all calls from the media are to be directed. If your run a small company, you might want to consider an outside agency or professional media consultant. Don't give the job to just anyone. It's not fair, because it requires someone with specialized skills. In the old days, a lot of companies directed such calls to the chief financial officer or the general counsel. But with the explosion of business media and the dynamics involved, CFOs are not experts in managing the new environment. Get a specialist.

In addition, alert your employees that if they receive calls from reporters to politely decline to talk to them and refer them to the point person. Remind them that even a "decline comment" is considered a comment, and that they should leave that decision to the person in charge of handling contacts with the press. What if it is an issue on which the company feels it wants to comment? What if it is an issue to which the company must respond? Explain to them that any conversation with a reporter, even if it's about the weather or last night's ball game, is an interview. And don't even begin to put conditions on this type of contact, such as on the record or off the record, or background or deep background. Most people, including many journalists, don't even understand what those terms mean, and many who do simply ignore them. The popular practice these days is for a reporter who wants to talk to an executive about a sensitive topic to suggest a background interview—which means the reporter can use the information but there can be no mention of the person interviewed or the company he or she represents. And no direct quotes. After the executive agrees, the reporter then comes back later and asks whether certain comments can be moved onto the record. If you decline, he throws a fit. Explaining that he or she can't change the rules after the game is over doesn't register. It is a sleazy trick. Beware.

When you have determined who your audiences are, how they want to receive their information, and what media vehicles to use, it is time to find the right spokespersons and train them to say the right things.

Determining the right thing to say is easier than convincing people of the need to learn to say it properly. Start with the basics about your company. What do you sell? What does your company stand for? Why do your customers choose your brand over your competitors'? What is your purpose for talking to the media about this? (Remember, growth strategy.) Use the answers to form the basis of every message you send to the media. In effect, tie every sound bite directly to your brand because in a noisy environment, people remember brands before they remember details. Finding the right spokesperson is an exercise in talent management. In the new media environment, there will be many opportunities. The trick is to choose the right person for the right opportunity. If you have them at your disposal, use a number of people. This will give the company many faces, appealing to many audiences. For example, set agendas for your senior people. Make sure the chief executive talks about strategic subjects. He or she should be the personality of the company, the visionary. Leave the nuts and bolts of products and processes to the heads of your business units.

If you can approach the new media environment methodically and resist the kid-in-a-candy-store syndrome, you will be on your way to building a solid and credible media profile. Do not feel pressured to do something you don't want to do if it doesn't make sense. Remember, you are the only one who can control your company's image. And in the chaotic, noisy new media environment, control is the key.

## Summary of Trends

▶ *In a media environment of plenty, companies are tempted to get as much publicity as they can.* But overexposure can be as damaging as not enough exposure.

▶ *The media is under so much pressure to fill space and time that they will chase almost any source.* The danger for credible sources is that there is a possibility of being lumped in with bad apples. It's not the bad apples who will suffer.

▶ *All publicity is not necessarily good, despite what certain celebrities say.* There is a difference between good publicity and bad publicity.

▶ *It is easy for companies to get caught up in the media explosion.* It is exciting and fun. In this environment, a star is born every minute. But your company wants more than just fifteen minutes of fame.

▶ *Audiences suffer from information overload or more precisely, disinformation overload.* When the facts run out and there's still space to fill, reporters will talk to anyone, including each other.

## Lessons for Companies

▶ *Be selective, be patient.* Don't be afraid to pass on media interview opportunities that don't fit your strategic objectives.

▶ *Start by making a list of media you consider to be credible or by updating your existing list.* Keep the list current. In the modern media environment, the movement of journalists between outlets is on the rise.

▶ *Find out how reporters on your list like to receive their information.* Understand how they like to do business with companies. You will win points.

▶ *Make sure your messages are focused and tied into your company's business strategy.* Make sure your media opportunities match your objectives.

▶ *Don't try to pass yourself off as something you are not.* Don't stretch your expertise. You will get caught. And if you get caught on national television, your credibility will be damaged forever.

▶ *Hire a public relations agency or consultant to help.* Make sure that a member of that team is a former journalist or a media relations specialist who knows how the media works.

▶ *Beware of public relations people who recommend media for media's sake.* Beware of the "hit" artist. The quality of the media opportunity is of paramount importance.

▶ *Beware of public relations "yes" men.* Demand counsel that is critical and constructive. Don't let your counselors get as close to the issue as you are. If they do, they lose their value. You need a foil, a sounding board. You're right a lot of the time, but not always.

# CHAPTER 10

# Above the Clatter

## What to Say and Who Should Say It

Jeff Bezos, the founder of the online retailer Amazon.com the online retailer, had a problem. Jacqueline Doherty, a tenacious reporter for *Barron's*, was reporting a story on the rapid decline in the company's stock—from $221 in April 1999 to almost half that, $118, by the end of May. The decline had cut the company's worth to about $19 billion, from $36 billion, and Bezos's personal fortune to $7 billion, from $13 billion. That's not a bad problem to have, when the downside leaves you a personal fortune worth $7 billion, but investors were beginning to wonder when this company, like so many other high-flying Internet offerings, would make some money. As Doherty wrote, "Unfortunately for Bezos, Amazon is now entering a stage in which investors will be less willing to rely on his charisma and more demanding of answers to tough questions like, when will this company actually turn a profit? And how will Amazon triumph over a slew of new competitors who have deep pockets and new technologies?"

They were fair questions, and because this is a growing public company with no track record, they needed to be answered. Because they were strategic in nature—in other words, they went right to the heart of the company's big plans for the future—it was up to the senior executive to respond. If ever there was an opportunity to reassure investors that a company was on track, this was it. Here was a chance, handed to Bezos on a silver platter, to lay out the company's strategy and to address, one by one, the criticisms leveled at Amazon.com.

But he passed. Not only did he decline to be interviewed, he also would not make available to the reporter any other Amazon executives. Not that this was a situation where anyone but the chief executive should speak. But he flatly denied any access whatsoever to the company's thinking.

He paid for it and in the process probably created a minor crisis for the company. The reporter wrote the article anyway, and it was devastating to the company and to him personally. Under the headline, "Amazon.Bomb—Investors Are Beginning to Realize That This Storybook Stock Has Problems," she led with a description of how Bezos's rise as a self-made Internet pioneer had lost its luster, and his honeymoon with investors had apparently ended. "Since early May," she wrote, "a lot of investors have been learning that a good story does not always make a good stock." Then— and here is the lesson—Doherty took Bezos himself to task for his failure to accept his responsibilities as the head of the company and to answer the pressing questions about the company's elusive profitability. "We tried to ask Bezos, but he declined to make himself or any other executives of the company available," Doherty wrote. "He can ignore *Barron's,* but he can't ignore the questions."

Whoever was giving Bezos public relations counsel is probably—or should be—out of a job. It is important not only to choose the people who speak for your company properly, but also to understand that in certain circumstances, especially if your company is under fire, it is important to have someone state your case. And in this situation, when an influential publication like *Barron's* calls, it's the chief executive who should answer. Not responding does a lot more than aggravate the reporter. The investors who have been asking the same questions get no answers. Neither do the investment community analysts who follow the company. And what do the company's employees think when they read a three-page feature article that has very little good to say and ends with this declaration: "Eventually, shareholders and bond buyers will wise up."

Worse, the company's refusal to cooperate caused two other things to happen: The holes in the story where Amazon's comments should have been were filled with speculation from outsiders. They were guessing at what the company was thinking, what it was up to. Was it correct or incorrect? Only the company knew for sure. How did the senior management expect investors to make informed decisions on speculation? The silence also raised the specter that there was something terribly wrong with the company. After all, the fact that it had not made a profit did not make it any different from almost every other Internet company in the world. By failing to acknowledge even that, the company stuck out like a sore, perhaps injured, thumb for investors.

## Picking the Right Spokesperson

Here's yet another situation that is not quite so damaging, yet underscores the importance of choosing spokespersons carefully and knowing how to use them effectively: A public relations colleague came to me once with a problem. He represented a major telephone company that was going through a merger, and his job was to help keep the media informed about how the systems of the two companies were being integrated. This was as big a task as the legal wrangling that went into the merger itself. Millions of customers, residential and business, were depending on seamless, uninterrupted service during the transition and wanted to know what the companies were going to do about it.

My friend's problem was ticklish. His client, the regional manager of one of the companies that had been put in charge of the integration, was not a good spokesman. Not that he didn't know his stuff. He could talk a blue streak and in great detail about connectivity, switches, trunks, and all the other technical stuff associated with the telecommunications business. If your phone went dead, this is the guy who knew how to fix it. He was so conscientious and energetic, he would probably come over to your house in the middle of the night to do it. The problem was he could not put the situation into layperson's terms, which is what most media need. The old rule of thumb is that daily newspapers write at a basic reading level so they don't confound their readers. That meant the writing had to be pretty simple and heavy on explanation as well as information. This guy could give only the information.

Adding to the dilemma was that he had been handpicked by the chairman of the company to be the spokesman for the task. He was so good at what he did—and obviously well liked by the people in both companies—that they considered him to be the obvious choice. Changing the way he was as a spokesman would be impossible, even with training. Finding a substitute who had the blessing of the chairman would be almost equally impossible.

Here's what we did. For a week, we videotaped every interview this regional manager conducted with the media. We edited the worst clips into a five-minute videotape and backed it up with a transcript. In effect, we built a case to convince the decision-makers on the project that things needed to change. Our motivation was not to be mean or unfair to this fellow. But we were concerned that because he was an ineffective spokesman, the key messages of the company were not being communicated clearly and the success of the project was in jeopardy.

After much maneuvering, we secured a meeting with the chairman and several other senior managers to present our findings. We explained to them the problem, being careful to praise the manager—he was good at his job, but not a good fit for this task. Then we showed the video. After only a minute or two, the chairman stopped us. He got the picture. We could choose and train a new spokesperson. There were no hard feelings toward the eager manager, but the success of the project was paramount.

## Senior Executives Have Their Limitations

It's one thing to face that problem with an employee well down the ladder, but what about when the spokesperson is the chief executive—and he's terrible? That was the case with one of my clients whose ego was so inflated it blinded him to the fact that when he went on television in advertisements and news interviews, not only was he difficult to understand, he made viewers uncomfortable. The man had a slight speech impediment and a noticeable accent. These were a deadly combination that hurt the reputation of the company because viewers turned him off.

Our recommendation was to limit him to print interviews, where there would be more opportunity for reporters to follow up with questions on issues that were not clear. And getting him off the airwaves would limit the other problems. Of course, the client did not take our advice. He continues to appear in his own ads and conduct television interviews. At the end of the day, it's his company. But it's also the responsibility of the media experts to alert their clients when something is wrong. Sometimes that truth hurts. Sometimes it is virtually impossible to tell the truth without hurting someone's feelings.

It is important to know your limitations, especially when it comes to representing your company in public. It is also important to know the strengths and weaknesses of all the people in your company who speak publicly about your business. Almost everyone is good at something, but few are good at everything. In the same way that it is important to match people's expertise and skills to their jobs, it is important to pick the appropriate people to say the appropriate things about your company.

There is another factor that makes the selection of spokespeople more difficult: Because business has become a personality business, and the movers and shakers have their own kind of celebrity, corporate public relations people have been replaced by senior executives as the main spokespersons for the company. The media doesn't really want to talk to someone in the middle unless it absolutely has to. As Bill Patterson, president of Reputation Management Associates in Columbus, Ohio, told PR Week magazine in January 1999, "In the old days, you didn't see the company president talking to the media. (You saw the PR pro.) But today, you don't see the Microsoft PR guy dealing with the media—it's Bill Gates himself. PR has become too important to be left to the PR department."

Let's think about that last statement. PR has become too important to be left to the PR department. As true as that may be, it has profound implications for companies. If, as Patterson correctly assumes, the media does not want to talk to the company flack anymore, the control of the messages is being passed to people who are not by definition experts in dealing with the media. The changing demands of the media have taken control out of the hands of the people best qualified to do the job and put them into the hands of those who either have no idea what to do or are terrified about dealing with the media. All of a sudden, these people become liabilities to themselves and to their companies. In effect, the public relations person at a company or the designated spokesperson at an outside agency has been relegated to the role of talent manager and, in some cases, trainer.

## The Need for Media Savvy

At the most fundamental level, this means there is a huge need for training executives to become media savvy. It means that for a company to regain control of its messages and the way they are delivered, the new media stars—the chief executives rather than the public relations people—must become comfortable taking heat from the media and learn to drive an agenda in an adversarial situation. To get to that point takes hard work— the communications people have to recreate senior executives in their own image in a relatively short period of time.

Before we look more closely at media training and message development, a couple of important points need to be made: First, talking to the media is a very different experience from talking at a meeting or a presentation, even with an audience of hundreds or thousands of people. Media training is a very different experience from so-called presentation training. Presentation training is valuable in that it teaches you not only to lay out your argument clearly and logically, but also to feel comfortable and confident in elaborating on points if questions are asked. But presentations almost always take place in a controlled environment. A sales meeting or an annual meeting has an agenda. Speakers speak, presenters present. Questions and answers follow, each questioner speaking one at time. The whole process is usually policed by a moderator who can cut off a questioner who rambles on too long or gets off the topic. The environment itself can be controlled, so training for such presentations concentrates on content.

The media environment, as we have seen, is far from controlled. There is no set agenda. Things do not proceed in order. Unless you are aggressive and push through your agenda, your messages may get lost. The media are so anxious to ask questions they have a problem letting most people get a word in edgewise. In addition, there is usually no moderator or meeting organizer who can step in and decide which questions are appropriate or limit the amount of time a questioner has. You have to do that yourself. Sometimes you have to be aggressive about it.

Adding to the stress is that often, especially in big, breaking stories, the environment in which you are delivering your messages to the media may not be all that comfortable. You may be corralled by a media mob outside a building on the street, on the courthouse steps, getting out of your car at a restaurant, or in the driveway of your own home. The setting may be noisy, distracting, and confusing. But when those bright camera lights go on and those microphones are stuck into your face, you have to perform. And you have to perform as if you were sitting in your office, calm and comfortable, with soft music playing and a cup of coffee at your side. People expect that of executives on television these days. Any sign of fear, confusion, or the inability to get a point across is considered by the media and their consumers to be a reflection of a problem in the company. You need to exude a confidence that tells people you are in charge, that the situation, whatever it may be, is under control. You know what you are doing.

When done properly, media training starts with all the skills of presentation training and then adds another set of skills for dealing with the crazy, unpredictable media environment in which executives must deliver their messages. Don't ever confuse the two. Presentation training is not media training. If you enter a media situation, especially a crisis, thinking that because you are a pretty good public speaker and you can get your point across with some slides or a Microsoft PowerPoint® presentation, you will be surprised at how really unprepared you are. And that lack of preparedness can have a serious impact on your company's reputation.

## Being Comfortable vs. Being Good at It

There's another problem companies often face when tackling the media training of their senior executives: I call it the "Been there, done that" syndrome. Executives who decline to have media training because they have participated in a few interviews are the most dangerous to the companies and themselves. Talking to the media a lot does not necessarily mean you are good at it. There is no direct link between the quantity of media contact you have and the quality you bring to it. There is a big difference between being comfortable in a media interview and being effective at delivering messages and driving an agenda. This is the most common mistake executives make. And it is hard for public relations counselors inside or outside a company to break this misconception. Who wants to tell a chief executive who has an ongoing contact with the media that he or she needs media training because the media interviews are not being handled effectively? It's like telling someone who's been driving a car for thirty years that he needs to take driving lessons because he's not really very good at it.

Here are a couple of examples: I had a client who was the chief executive of a major retail company. He was a wonderful guy—charming, funny, self-deprecating, and brutally honest about what's good and bad about the world. In addition, he was a self-made man, so he had a homespun charm that endeared him to people. The media, like almost everyone else, loved him. And so did the analysts who followed the company. His media interviews were like fireside chats, with long rambling anecdotes about wins and losses, childhood fantasies, and hopes and dreams. His conference calls with analysts were much the same. He would ride tangents to the very end, spinning wonderful yarns that would have these hard-bitten number-crunchers enraptured. He was, in the

purest sense, an old-fashioned storyteller. And therein lay the problem from a communications point of view. While he was extremely
effective at capturing the imagination of the audiences he was
speaking to, he was terrible at delivering key messages and answering pointed questions about the company's strategy, which was
really what these people wanted to know. He would wrap whatever strategic messages he wanted to convey so heavily in anecdotes and stories that the listeners either missed the point or gave
up trying to find it. It was too much work. He was the type of fellow
who, if asked for the time, would not simply tell you how a clock is
made, but how when he was a boy he met a peculiar watchmaker
in a small Swiss village who, though blind, produced some of the
most beautiful, intricately tooled timepieces in the world.

At the same time, he was terrible at giving listeners, especially analysts, a serious vision of the future. When asked what he
saw happening in the coming year, he would fall into the same
trap. "Who can tell," he would say. "Did Columbus know what
lay ahead of him when he set out to find the new world? All he
knew was that there was a new world out there somewhere, and
he wasn't even sure about that." Interesting point, but not helpful to analysts whose job it is to provide clients with some forward-looking thinking. And any analyst who based future
assumptions on the Columbus theory would be laughed out of
the business. But there was a more serious problem than the analysts' reputations: This executive could not or would not articulate
a vision or even speculate about industry trends he thought
might affect his business. People thought he had no idea at all
what was going on. After all, if he had a handle on the future, he
would say it, wouldn't he? The doubts about whether he really
had a clear idea about what was going on hurt him. One analyst
likened him to her aging grandfather: "You love to curl up beside
him and listen to his stories, but after a while, you realize that he
has no idea what he's talking about."

The kicker, of course, is that this client refused to be media
trained, even though we made a very strong case to support the
recommendation. His response was, "I talk to the media all the

time. Why on earth would I need training?" He was caught in his own blind spot, believing that the mere practice of talking to the media meant that he was a good communicator. It was folly, and it was a disappointment because he had enormous intelligence and presence. He was a media trainer's dream—charismatic, witty, friendly, charming. All of these attributes were wasted because he could not see his own limitations and would not take counsel about them. Unfortunately for communicators, a lot of self-made executives are like this. They have done it their way, and it has worked. Why, they ask, should handling the media be any different? Well, it is.

## The Importance of Media Training

Practice makes perfect. Athletes, even at the top of their game, practice. They work out, they train. After all the countless hours they have spent getting to where they are, they do not stop. They need to keep their skills sharp. They need to stay in shape. They need to keep up with changes in the rules, changes in nuances of the competition, changes in how their rivals play the game. Executives are no different. As an executive, you are constantly keeping in shape about your company's competitive position and your customers' needs. If you're smart, you are constantly pushing yourself and your company to new levels of management skills, driving to be better, to be the best. The game of communications is no different. And, I suggest, it has become such an important part of a company's business strategy that it is dangerous not get in shape for it. Or, if you are in shape, it is dangerous to stop training and get flabby. With the media environment changing so quickly, and with technology putting your company in the public eye all the time, you cannot afford to let the gap between your skill level and the level required to compete successfully get too wide.

   The best in the business have learned that. Mary Farrell, a senior market strategist at PaineWebber, for example, is the last person anyone would think needs media training. She appears on television regularly as a commentator on CNBC, and in the print media. She is in great demand among producers for network evening news shows and morning programs. She is a regular guest on the popular PBS business program, "Wall Street Week" with Louis Rukeyser, and, in fact, was handpicked by him to host the show when he is out of town or on vacation. In addition, she is constantly on the road, giving seminars to packed houses of brokers, clients, and prospective clients. You might say that the better part of Farrell's life is spent in the public eye. And you might think that because of that, she would not need media training, or if told she needed it, would decline.

But not only does she understand the value of media training, she asks for it. Like any good professional, she works hard to stay at the top of her game. She doesn't simply perform and forget about it. She reviews what she has said, how she has said it, how the audiences she addressed reacted to her messages. She looks for strengths to leverage, weaknesses to improve, new ideas to make her more effective. During one of these reviews, she asked our media group to help her hone her skills.

She was worried that while she was answering questions, that's all she was doing. She was not taking the questions and giving them her perspective. She was not injecting into the answers enough of the forward-looking strategic advice for which she was known. Perhaps it was because when plopped in a chair under bright lights in a television studio, it was easy to feel reactive rather than proactive. It was an interesting nuance, but an important one. Farrell needed to be more than simply a font of information—she needed to be a credible dispenser of insight and opinion. The audiences, particularly the consumer-investors who watched business television, demanded it.

So, we worked with her to develop messages that were more strategic and prepared questions and answers that would test her ability to raise her interviewing techniques to a high level. And we hired a professional media trainer to come in and help. Working with a media trainer is a valuable, if humbling, experience. If you think you're pretty good with the media, spend a couple of hours with a good professional media trainer and you will learn that you may not be as good as you think. Media training sessions, unless they are highly focused on a specific issue and a specific media outlet, usually test a communicator's skills in all the common interviewing methods—telephone, face-to-face, on-camera, and, increasingly, online. The good trainers conduct mock interviews with the subject, trying as best they can to recreate the environments in which such an interview occurs. They will bring their own camera equipment, complete with hot lights. They will bring their own tape recorders with a handheld broadcast microphone that they will stick in the subjects' faces. The really good ones will do their homework. They will get as much information as they can about the issues facing the company and the critical press the company has received, and they will prepare lines of questioning that are very pointed and relevant, not generic. The sessions can be very effective if the preparation is sufficient and the subject is convinced enough about the value of the process to take it seriously. For a joker who thinks he knows it all, and finds role-playing an uncomfortable activity, it is a waste of time. If you are serious about this, take your lead from Mary Farrell. She worked hard to prepare for the media training session and worked during the simulations. She wanted to be a better communicator, even though she was already one of the top communicators in the business. The result of her efforts is that she has improved her skills as a counselor to investors, offering insight as well as information. She has taken more control of the situation, assuming a less reactive and more reactive stance in interviews. She has learned to drive an agenda, not simply respond to someone else's. The best has become even better. The lesson is clear.

## It Takes Hard Work

And as valuable as Farrell's story is, there is an even better one—a personal favorite of mine—that should prove to doubters that making it look easy takes hard work. At the risk of overloading this discussion with sports metaphors, I will point once again to professional athletes as a set-up. If you think that people like basketball star Michael Jordan, football star Jerry Rice, or any other athlete who has reached the pinnacle of his sport achieves what he has achieved on pure talent, you are wrong. The talent may have gotten these athletes noticed, but it's the hard work they do every day that keeps them there. The same is true for communicators, in every line of business.

In the winter of 1998, I took a client to appear on "The Charlie Rose Show," a popular PBS program with an unusual format in today's world of television glitz. The interviewer, Charlie Rose, sits at a plain wooden table across from his guest. The set has a jet black backdrop—with no fancy graphics—and subtle lighting. The only props are Rose's coffee cup, and perhaps one for his guest, and a book or two. The interviews are usually one-on-one, though on occasion there are three at the table and perhaps another piped in on video. But the group discussions are the exception. The power and effectiveness of the show is its intimacy, its lack of distraction. Everything is focused on the subject. The program lasts for half an hour, without commercial interruption. It is not a sound bite environment. It is an interview in the traditional sense—a discussion, a conversation

For guests, this is an appealing format, though it can be intimidating, especially for those who are used to delivering their key messages in a matter of seconds to interviewers who are not close to the issue. And Rose is a thorough interviewer. He digs deep into the lives of his subjects, finding out what has been said or written about them, learning what makes them tick, understanding their likes and dislikes. It is not uncommon for guests to stop and respond, "How on earth did you know that? You really did do your homework." Rose also has a very effective interviewing technique that is perfectly suited to the format. He will ask a question, listen to the answer, and then wait. He will not immediately jump back into the discussion with a follow-up question. He will muse about the answer for a minute, rub his chin with his hand. Untrained guests, already a little nervous about their appearance, often make the mistake of filling the space. It's the same human reaction to a pregnant pause in a conversation. The silence is so uncomfortable, people feel the need to fill it. And if they fill it for Charlie Rose, he has achieved what he wanted—his guests start to talk more about issues and themselves and stop answering questions. Of course, some guests end up telling him more than they thought they would, but that's what makes it great television.

The point is, guests of Charlie Rose should be prepared. It is not a typical interview. But because of the unique format, it is a popular and therefore important program. So when I arrived with my client, we were prepared. He had studied his key messages. He knew his subject cold, and he was quite skilled at media appearances. We had briefed him on the format of the program and alerted him to Rose's penchant for digging up unexpected details and his "pregnant pause" interviewing technique. We had watched tapes of previous shows to get a real sense of what the experience would be all about.

Just as my client was about to go into the studio, the door to the green room opened and in walked the comic Joan Rivers, accompanied by two assistants. She arrived with a flourish and quickly introduced herself. She was friendly and energetic. I was a little concerned that she would be a distraction for my client, even though they would not appear together on camera. He was a laid back fellow, not a movie or television star. And I thought Rivers, as a personality, would disrupt the entire operation.

I was dead wrong. In fact, I quickly learned what it takes to be a real professional. After introducing herself, Rivers sat down with her assistants, and they all pulled out notebooks. For the next twenty minutes, they engaged in one of the most intensive briefing sessions I have ever witnessed. Were these messages valid? Did we check these facts? Is the delivery of this joke or this line O.K.? Should we turn it around and approach it from a different way? Is this too outrageous to say or not outrageous enough? I must have been staring, and perhaps my mouth was a little agape, because at one point about halfway through their discussion, Rivers stopped the conversation and looked up at me. "I'm sorry," she said, "Are we being too loud? We get a little intense when we're working." That's right, working. For all of you—and I include myself in this category—who think being funny is easy, it's not. It's the same reason that dunking a basketball isn't easy, catching a fifty-yard touchdown pass isn't easy, and hitting a ninety-five-mile-an-hour fastball isn't easy. It's hard work. And Joan Rivers, who makes it look easy, works hard to make it look easy. When she appeared a few minutes later on camera, she was fabulous. She was prepared, she was funny, she was charming. She was, from long before the lights came up until the cameras had stopped rolling, the consummate professional.

These anecdotes, I believe, tell the important lessons about media training and the selection of the appropriate people to do the talking for your company. You can buy several good books that are devoted to the techniques of media training, including message development, training techniques, even learning how to groom and dress the part to exude the most credibility, or style, or pizzazz. But to get to the stage where you can actually use that information, you have to reach the stage in your organization where everyone understands the value of the practice. That is a far more difficult task than the training itself. And it is something young and mature companies alike must tackle. If you are the public relations person in charge of the talent management of the company, try to use some sports metaphors to make your point, if they are appropriate, and the executives in question will respond. But don't restrict yourself to sports metaphors. Pick anyone who has become the best in his or her field, and use that person as an example. The best got to be there because they worked hard. And they stay where they are because they work even harder.

If you are an executive who is a spokesperson, has been chosen to be a spokesperson, or would like to be one, take this advice. No matter how much you think you know about the media, you can always know more. No matter how good you think you are as a communicator, you can always do better. Get trained. Allow PR specialists to help hone your messages, improve your style. If you are the chief executive, have your senior people go through training, too, even if you don't anticipate that they will talk to the media much. In a crisis, if you or other designated spokespeople are not available, it is a great insurance policy to have a backup who is trained to do the job.

And don't make training a one-time event. Keep your skills fresh. Brush up on your techniques regularly. Use a big announcement or event to practice, with a trainer. And keep aware of the different reporting techniques being developed by the media. In this changing environment, you cannot afford to fall behind on the knowledge curve. Know the rules and how they are changing. If you do all this, you will become a more effective communicator. You will know who should respond in a certain situation, what they should say, and how they should say it. The benefits for the company will be tangible. The downside of continuing to be an ineffective communicator will be tangible, too, even if you have lots of exposure. Remember, in today's media environment, anyone can get exposure. But not everyone knows how to make the most of it. You should learn.

## Summary of Trends

▶ *The growth of the business media has changed the roles of company spokespeople.* The media no longer wants to talk to the traditional spokespeople—the public relations people. They want to talk directly to the decision-makers—the senior management.

▶ *Control of the management of a company's public face has been transferred from public relations to senior management.* The problem: Most senior managers are not trained as spokespeople. They don't know how to prioritize; they don't know how to act.

▶ *The public relations function has become an exercise in talent management.* With this shift in control, public relations people must transfer their media skills to senior executives, in effect creating them in their own image.

▶ *The media environment is not a meeting or presentation environment.* It is not controlled, there is no agenda, and there is no moderator. It is a free-for-all. Therefore, presentation training is not effective as a preparatory method for media work. Don't be fooled.

▶ *The methods used by the media are changing regularly and rapidly.* Techniques that were used a year ago may not be in vogue any more.

## Lessons for Companies

▶ *Understand the need to be prepared.* Know the power and the value of training spokespersons and the dangers of not training them.

▶ *Get rid of your ego when it comes to media relations and training.* You may think you are a great communicator, but even great communicators need some help from time to time. You could probably use some, too. Remember, the stars in all fields work hard to keep their skills sharp.

▶ *Get outside professional help.* Trainers can hone messages, run simulations, teach you how to take control of media situations. The goal is to set the agenda in a media interview, not to be simply reactive.

▶ *Train all your important people, including those who do not work with the media a lot.* In a crisis, or in the event of a big announcement, you can use some bench strength.

▶ *Incorporate media training into your regular, ongoing management training programs.* Make it compulsory for anyone in your company who deals with the media. Your company's image will benefit.

# CHAPTER 11

# Know the Enemy
## The Chink in the PR Armor

I n the summer of 1998, a sensational sex scandal rocked Wall Street and tested the public relations skills of some of the best in the business. They pretty much failed, because they didn't understand how the media thinks, how the media acts, and what makes a news story compelling. Public relations professionals and their strategists must not only understand what you as a client want to say—they must also anticipate the environment into which your messages will be sent.

The situation began when a prominent investment banker was sued by his girlfriend, a model and actress roughly fifty years his junior. The basis of the lawsuit was simple and emotionally charged: The girlfriend claimed that in exchange for her many years of companionship, the banker had promised to marry her and support her financially in the style to which she had become accustomed. Well, at this point, marriage was out of the question for two reasons: He was already married and, the suit alleged, he had dumped the girlfriend in favor of one of her twentysomething friends. The "hell hath no fury" syndrome began, and after a settlement failed, the girlfriend sued the banker for $3.5 million. She also went to the press—namely *The New York Post* and *The New York Daily News*.

For the tabloids, the story wrote itself. Sex, money, power, adultery. And the night before it broke, I got a call from the banker and his lawyer, giving me a so-called heads-up about the situation. Reporters had called, they told me. One had even sent a photographer to the banker's Connecticut mansion. For these reasons, they said, there might be a "little item" in the papers the next day, and as the firm's spokesman for the firm, I might get "a couple of calls." As they gave me more details, I told them I thought they had grossly miscalculated the situation. The *Daily News* and the *Post* did not dispatch reporters and photographers for a brief item. Considering the salacious elements of the story, I suggested it would get bigger play than they expected. They didn't believe me. But I immediately informed the senior management of the firm that the morning papers would bring some embarrassing, though not particularly fatal, exposure for the firm.

The next day was worse than what I had imagined. The *Daily News* ran the story on page one with a photo of the girlfriend under the headline, "Russian Beauty Slams Wall St. Exec with $3.5M Sex Suit. Ex-Model Says Tycoon Dumped Her for Another Mistress After 9 Years." Inside, there was a two-page spread, with photos, under the headline, "She has a trysted tale. Says Wall St. sugar daddy dumped her." The collage of photos included a snapshot of the banker and the woman hugging and a picture of the banker's house in Connecticut where, the caption noted, he lived with his wife.

The *New York Post* topped all that. Its front-page headline, "The Kinky Tycoon," was accompanied by photographs of the banker and his girlfriend. Inside, on a two-page spread, the headline read, "Dumped Mistress Sues XXX-Tycoon," with a glamor shot of the girlfriend in tight jeans, rear end to the camera. There was even a separate story quoting the banker's wife under the headline, "Wife Defends Mr. Moneybags," with a photo of the wife in the driveway of the couple's home.

As embarrassing as it was for all involved, it was not really a business story. And the firm really had no reason to comment since the activities outlined in the lawsuit were not even remotely related to the business the banker did for the firm. Still, we were flooded with requests for comment from more than eighty media outlets.

Later in the day, the banker called me with a request. Would

I act as his spokesman, since I seemed to understand how the media would react? I was flattered, but declined. I told him I could not act as both a spokesman for the firm and a spokesman for him because it was important to make clear to the public that this issue was a personal issue that did not relate to the firm. He understood, but was worried. He no longer believed that his lawyer was the appropriate person to be handling the media strategy for the situation, and I agreed. I suggested a couple of things. If I were he, I said, I would go on a two-week vacation with my wife, and get out of the glare. This was a one-day story, in that there was probably not much more to tell. And since it was a tabloid story for the most part, they would probably be on to some other scandal the next day. By the time he returned, it would be forgotten. Besides, staying in town would simply expose him and his family to more questions and embarrassment. My other suggestion was to talk to a personal publicist, a public relations professional who specialized in handling personal publicity and image management for high-profile people. Such a person, I suggested, would probably have more creative ideas than fleeing town on how to minimize the damage.

Whether the banker ever sought this kind of help, I'm not sure. For the sake of the public relations profession, I hope he didn't. Because what appeared in the papers the next day made a bad situation even worse. Both the *Daily News* and *The New York Post* ran articles saying that an elderly couple, disguised in baseball caps and sunglasses, had been seen in a Connecticut town buying up all the newspapers at stores, newsstands, street boxes, and commuter train stations. While there was no evidence that it was the banker and his wife, there was little doubt about it. The articles were merciless, making fun of the couple for the stunt and, even worse, retelling the whole sordid tale of the scandal in the process. If the banker had received that advice from a public relations professional, he should have withheld payment. If he got the idea from a friend, it was bad advice. And if he came up with the scheme himself, well, desperate times demand desperate measures.

# Be Prepared: Understand Reporters

The point is clear. To compete in business, you have to know your competitor as well as you know yourself. It is no different with the media. To handle a reporter, you have to think like one. This is where most public relations people fail miserably. They don't understand a reporter's agenda. They don't know the angle of a story. You may be surprised that a lot of them don't even read a newspaper every day. There is no mystery in finding out what a reporter is driving at. But you don't want to find out in the middle of an interview. It takes homework.

Demand that your media relations people do their homework diligently. You demand the same of your lawyers, your product people, and your sales force. Find out what stories the reporters have been working on. What issues interest them? How have they approached their beat? Read their articles. Watch video clips of their programs. If your people can't do it, there are consulting services that provide a wealth of information. Among the best is the TJFR Group in Denver. For a fee, it will supply not only biographical information on reporters but also insight into their reporting styles and approaches.

Technology, which has become the business journalist's most powerful weapon, can become yours, too. Everything that has been written about or generated by your company for public consumption is at a reporter's disposal almost instantly through any number of data bases. A reporter probably knows things about your company you don't even remember. But all this information is available to your company, too.

The lesson here is be a good Boy Scout. Be prepared. Have at least as much technology and information as the reporter you are dealing with. Spend the money. Buy the systems. It is stupid to risk the reputation of your entire company to save a few dollars.

Arming yourself with the same information is only part of the challenge. The real task is to understand what the media is going to do with it. I am constantly surprised by executives who, despite the fact that they follow the media regularly and often talk with reporters, remain mystified about why reporters write what they write. In reality, these executives are mystified about why reporters don't write what companies tell them to write.

## What Motivates Reporters?

To understand what goes into a reporter's agenda, you must understand his or her motivations. And while it is dangerous and unfair to generalize, there are some basics that are pretty much universal. At least, they were for me during my twenty years as a journalist. The first is that what the journalist does is not in any way related to the commerce of the media outlet to which he or she is attached. Business people have a hard time understanding that a reporter is not motivated by the desire to make money for the newspaper or television or radio station. That's why one of the main things I tell business people who are dealing with the media is never kid a reporter that what he or she is writing "will sell a lot of papers." It is a common mistake among business people, and they actually think it is a compliment. They believe that reporters are rewarded, both by their bosses and through self-satisfaction, if the stories they write make money. In effect, hot stories do contribute to the bottom line. A good story played prominently will generate interest and prompt people to buy more papers. But reporters and editors do not care. For many of them, the suggestion that they are writing stories to generate revenues for their company is an insult.

Here's what business people who deal with reporters need to understand: Most reporters consider themselves craftspeople, artisans, writers. If they are in television, they may consider themselves personalities or budding stars. The fact that they have to sell their talents to a commercial enterprise to put food on the table and pay the rent is the downside of the business. They would far prefer that there was a distinct separation of church and state—church being the sanctity of journalism and state being the money-grubbing side of the business of journalism. In many ways, media companies take advantage of a journalist's talent.

With a few exceptions—the multimillion-dollar anchor personalities and television stations come to mind—journalists are relatively poorly paid, even those in the highest editorial ranks of
major outlets and those with post-graduate degrees. What would
possess someone to pay for an MBA to land a job that pays
$40,000 or less at a media outlet? On top of that, with news
available twenty-four hours a day, seven-days a week, the hours
are long and the schedules merciless. Most normal people would
not want the job even if it paid more money. But for a salary that
in New York City will barely pay the rent, why bother?

The answer is the clue to everything you need to know
about the media. Reporters really believe that their purpose in this
world is to seek out the truth and tell everybody about it. I'm not
kidding. They are convinced that what they are doing as watch-
dogs or sounding boards is the purest of pursuits and therefore
should be untainted with commercial concerns. Reporters don't
simply want to know, they want to know the truth. The average
reader needs protection from the lies and deceit of the big bad
world. They need help determining what's real, what's not,
what's right, and what's wrong. As one friend of mine said to me
when I was working the overnight shift as a young reporter in
Toronto for about $20,000 a year: "I'm all for noble causes, but
this is ridiculous."

But a noble cause it is, or at least from the journalist's point
of view. Reporters take their responsibility very seriously—some a
little too seriously. I remember sitting in a news meeting at *The
New York Times* when the discussion turned to a feature story
about a company that had been lying to its customers about a
hazardous product. The fact that the product was used by young
children made the story a particularly emotional one. The company had taken its knocks. Consumer groups were outraged,
retailers had pulled the products from their shelves, and customers were demanding refunds. The company's stock had
tanked. The sheepish senior executives, who at first made a public relations blunder by denying that the product was defective,
eventually came clean and admitted the problem. They even

apologized. The article we were preparing traced the problem and how it was discovered. And again, because there were children involved, it took on an extra emotional element. During part of the discussion in the meeting about the company's denial and failed coverup, one of the senior editors put down her pen and said, "It's obvious, isn't it? This company is evil."

The rest of us were a little startled, since this was after all just a business, despite the fact that children had been killed or injured by its products. But she was adamant. "This company is evil. And we have to tell people not just about what they've done, but about how evil their motivations were." Now, there are a lot of strange people in the world, and some of them run businesses. But to make the jump from a company making a mistake to branding it as evil is a dangerous proposition. But this incident gives some insight into the passion with which most journalists, especially at the big outlets, approach their work.

## Keeping the Editorial Side Independent

Another common mistake business executives make when dealing with media concerns the reporter's motivations. Some business people still believe that if they are advertisers with a media outlet such as a newspaper, the newspaper's reporters should print whatever their company says. Tom Brigham, president of Brigham Scully Inc. in Woodland Hills, California, put his finger directly on the problem in an article in which he participated in the October 1994 issue of the American Management Association's *Management Review* magazine. Many CEOs, he said, "think of PR as, 'Let's send a press release and, damn it, we advertise so they ought to run it.' They don't understand what real public relations is, or even what real solid press relations is." Again, the mistake made by these executives is in thinking that the editorial agenda is directly linked to the business agenda of a newspaper. At good newspapers, the business side understands the importance of keeping the editorial side independent for several reasons. Among the most important: Readers buy a newspaper expecting news that is impartial—they do not buy it because it is a mouthpiece for companies or politicians or celebrities. They entrust the reporters and editors with the responsibility of cutting through the fluff and bluster, and delivering as true a picture of a situation as possible. And the reporters take this role very seriously. Most reporters believe readers have a right to get the truth from the newspapers they read.

## Seeking the Truth and Telling a Good Tale

Readers pay money every day expecting their newspapers to tell them the truth without sugar-coating it. The other reason that smart newspapers—and other media outlets, I should add—keep editorial and business sides separate is that it helps them attract good journalists. Remember, a deep motivator of responsible journalists is a work environment that is as free of conditions as possible. After all, the truth is unconditional, despite what lawyers may mean when they use the term "true fact." So why shouldn't the pursuit of truth be unconditional as well? If a newspaper has the reputation for editorial integrity, good journalists will flock to it, even for poor pay and long hours. Business people need to understand that to understand a reporter's agenda.

It will not surprise you to know that when a reporter is competing against another reporter from a rival outlet on the same story, the last thing on his mind is whether his story is going to sell more papers for his company than the other reporter's story will sell for his. They could not care less. The goal is to get the better story with the better information and the more credible sources to back it up. In other words, the goal is to get truth that is better than your competitor's truth. For those who consider themselves writers as well a reporters—a rarified standing among their peers—another motivation is their need to come up with a catchy lead paragraph and nice turns of phrase.

One of my favorite stories that illustrates this point occurred in the late 1980s, when a peculiar event emerged out of a small town in the Northeast. A local lottery winner, it seemed, had

blown all his cash with frightening speed and had virtually nothing to show for it, in material terms, at least. Reporters who followed the story found him sitting on the same bar stool in the
same dingy bar where he hung out only months before when he
was unemployed and penniless. He was still wearing rumpled
clothes and had not improved any aspects of his personal appearance or hygiene despite his riches. But he was happy, which confused a lot of the young reporters who simply thought he was
crazy. The big question, of course, was how did he spend several
million dollars in only a few months without improving his lot, by
many people's standards anyway. It was not in a Swiss bank, and
his friends, the townspeople, had seen him spending the money.
The answer was quite simple. He had bought drinks and dinner
for several months straight for everyone—including himself—who
came into his favorite watering hole, and visited a prostitute on a
regular basis. Oh, and he took a ride on an airplane once because
he had never been on one. The remainder of the money he had
given to friends and charities and, well, he couldn't really remember what else he did with it.

Many of the reporters were stunned. It was a good, if peculiar,
story. In fact, it was good because it was peculiar. And everyone
began to write and report on it. One reporter, though, rose above
them all because of his writing prowess, and earned the respect of
his peers (though no more money) with this lead paragraph: "Mil-
lionaire lottery winner [John Doe] spent most of his money on fast
women and cheap booze. The rest he spent foolishly."

The competitive juices of reporters get going not because of
the prospect of filling their newspaper's coffers but because they
have the chance to give their readers a better story, a better version of the truth, and if they have skill, the opportunity to tell a
nice tale in the process. In the end, gratification usually comes in
the knowledge that a reporter has "beaten" a rival, produced a
better story, fulfilling the obligations of the relationship the newspaper has with its readers.

In many other businesses, a job well done is often accompanied by a little something extra in the paycheck. It is rare in jour-

nalism. A note from an editor or a publisher saying "nice job" is often the only acknowledgment. A call from a reader to express gratitude is gravy. Once I called a reporter friend of mine to congratulate her on a story she had written. She was flattered and thankful. "And you know what," she said, "They gave me a hundred bucks for it." She was not being facetious. This money was unexpected, unnecessary, though thoroughly appreciated. For most reporters, though, the real thrill can come on a crowded subway car, when they see someone—a complete stranger—reading the story they have written under their bylines. It is heady stuff for the average reporter.

## The All-Important Byline

Another glimpse into the motivations of journalists, particularly print journalists, is that they're obsessed with bylines. Most people in business don't even look to see who wrote a story, probably thinking what the story says is more important. But for journalists, the first thing they look at is the byline of the writer. It is more than just a name, it is the author's signature. Like the artist's name painted on canvas, a byline is a reporter's most important point of recognition. It tells the world—or so they think—that this is their work, their truth. It says trust me, because I put my name on it. This may sound funny to the average business executive but consider that you protect your name and the name of your company the same way. It is your brand. A reporter's byline is his brand. It is actually more important than the name of the newspaper itself, even if the newspaper is *The New York Times*.

It is no wonder, then, that competition for bylines is so intense. It is the most important point of recognition for reporters, even beyond the paycheck. Reporters fight to have their bylines on stories. For young reporters, their first bylined story is considered a rite of passage and cause for celebration. It is recognition that what you say and how you say it is worthy of print, and the newspaper for whom you work trusts you enough to allow you to put your brand with their brand. On stories with more than one reporter, the proper hierarchy of the byline is an important and often difficult process to unravel. *The New York Times* even has style peculiarity that governs nuances in double bylines—where two reporters are named. The use of the word "and" to link the reporters' names is different from using the word "with" to link them. Does the average reader understand or care? Absolutely not. But to the reporters involved, and their rivals as well, it is of the utmost importance. It tells the small world of people who pay attention to these things how much work you did and, presumably, your position in the pecking order.

There is a peculiar, though not widespread phenomenon at some media outlets that companies need to be aware of. It is the practice of forcing reporters to compete against each other for stories. The editors involved choose the best story and run it under the "winning" reporter's byline. It's a dirty trick and hard on morale. If you consider what motivates reporters, this practice is akin to a vote of no-confidence for the loser of the battle. It is an indication that the powers that be do not consider a reporter's work worthy of the paper. They do not believe that the reporter's brand belongs on the same page with that of the newspaper. No amount of money would make the practice palatable to the average reporter. Yet, it goes on at the highest levels.

While I was the corporate spokesman at PaineWebber, I saw the practice in action. At the time, PaineWebber and about thirty other major Wall Street firms were involved in a settlement of claims of irregularities in over-the-counter trading. Despite what the regulators seemed to say, it appeared that what was a common industrywide practice at the time was deemed illegal or at least inappropriate under the new rules of the business. It was, in effect, a case of hindsight justice. Still, many of the firms involved had taken internal steps to restructure their over-the-counter operations to comply with the new rules and adapt to the new business environment that had resulted. People had left firms, and new ones had been hired. The story was of interest to the media because the combined settlement was worth a billion dollars. It was big money, and there were claims in the government's case that indicated wrongdoing against clients.

Most responsible companies in the middle of litigation, do not talk about settlements or any aspects of the case, which of course angered the media. Reporters were scrambling to get information, but Wall Street was buttoned up pretty tightly—pretty amazing for an industry in which leaks are a common occurrence. The frustration level grew among the reporters seeking information about the possible size of the settlement and the allegations that were apparently supporting the government's case. The reporter who was covering the story for *The Wall Street Journal* called me and our general counsel several times a day. There were no hard feelings about the incessant calls. He was doing his job, and we were doing ours. Then, in the midst of the action, our general counsel took a phone call from another *Journal* reporter, a senior investigative reporter who did not cover the beat. He had known the general counsel for years and tried to use that relationship as leverage. There was nothing wrong with the practice—reporters are trained to use relationships to get information in the same way companies and public relations executives use relationships with reporters to disseminate information. The general counsel, during his conversation with the reporter, told him that despite the relationship, there was not much he could do to help. Besides, he said, he really couldn't help one reporter and not help the other reporter working on the story.

After the conversation, the general counsel came to me scratching his head. "Did you know," he asked, "that they've got someone else on the story? I just got a call from him." The news did not surprise me. Having worked on enough big stories during my life as a journalist, I knew the team approach was common and preferred. It was good information to know, especially because the number and caliber of reporters involved give you some insight into how vigorously the story is being pursued and how prominently it will be played. (Remember the lesson learned from the investment banker's sex scandal—the *New York Post* and the *New York Daily News* don't dispatch teams of reporters and photographers if they're planning to write brief items.) But, we agreed, the fact that more than one reporter was working on this story was not cause for alarm, even if one of those involved was considered to be one of the paper's "big guns."

I thought nothing more about it until I received yet another call from the regular reporter on our beat who was checking in one more time to see if the situation had changed and whether anyone at the firm could give him some help. I chuckled, only because the exchange of useless phone calls—for both sides— had reached absurd proportions. "Listen," I cajoled him, "We can't say anything to you. And you can tell your friend at the desk across from you that we can't say anything to him, so he can quit calling our lawyers." The phone line went silent. "What friend across the desk?" he asked. "Have they got him working on this story?" It was immediately apparent that he was in the dark. As the lead reporter on the beat, he thought he was the lone wolf, or at least the lead wolf on the story. He probably assumed that he would get some support from younger reporters and researchers, but a big name would threaten his byline. Why hadn't anyone told him?

Why editors don't tell reporters these things is unclear. But it happens all the time, and when it does, companies need to beware. Competition among reporters at rival outlets is enough of a problem. But when a reporter learns, by accident, that he is competing against a colleague—especially a high profile one—it threatens the relationship the company has with the reporter in question. I felt sorry for this fellow, having seen it happen a thousand times during my career in journalism. But there was nothing I could do. I could not give him anything more than I had already given him, which was nothing, without jeopardizing the firm and, ultimately, my job. Yet, he pressed harder, angry with the situation. In effect, his problem became my problem and, in turn, the firm's problem. He could yell and scream at his editors, but it would not solve the problem. The only thing that would redeem him would be to get information, to get the best truth he could, and hope that it was better truth than his big-gun colleague could get. In the end, neither of them got anything. In fact, no one in the media got very much at all. But the situation had tested, indeed strained, the relationship between us and both of the reporters.

## Closing the Information Gap Through Technology

A final piece of guidance on understanding reporters' agendas: Don't underestimate their drive and ability to get information about you and your company, especially in an era with more technological wonders at their fingertips. While there is a talent deficit associated with the new business media explosion, inexperienced reporters are able to close the information gap more quickly than ever before. That is what drives them toward the truth. The more information they can get, the more people they can talk to, the better their reporting of the truth. A reporter friend of mine is so tenacious, she routinely gathers three or four more times the information than she actually uses in a story. Her feeling is that if you cast your net wide enough, you are bound to gather in a prize catch or two. And what used to take her days to gather—searching clipping files, newspaper morgues, company reports—now takes her a matter of hours. With data bases and the Internet, the time it takes for a reporter to get from nothing to something—from speculation to the truth—has been compressed. And the information is better, more complete, and more up to date.

Companies that believe the only things that reporters know are what their senior executives tell them are horribly mistaken. They must understand that a reporter has at his or her fingertips the technology to confirm or blow holes in the information you provide almost instantaneously. Technology has, in many cases, put reporters ahead of companies. A client of mine was embarrassed once when a reporter called to ask questions about his company's proxy statement, which the reporter pulled down from the Securities and Exchange Commission's electronic database, Edgar, before the company's legal department had distributed the final version to the senior managers and the corporate spokesperson. In the end, there was no harm done, but there were a few red faces. Another reason to beware.

Here's a little tidbit that you won't learn in any public relations textbook, but it is an important part of building and maintaining relationships with reporters. It shows them that you understand something about what motivates them. It's easy and will cost you only the price of a stamp. From time to time, drop a reporter a note, handwritten, commenting on a story they have written. The note is a personal touch, especially useful and unique in an era when print reporters and others spend most of their waking hours in front of computer terminals. The story doesn't have to be about your company. In fact, if it is about a company, industry or issue that is not in any way related to your own, even better. The fact that you read the piece will indicate to the reporter that you follow his or her work, and the story was so interesting that it caught your eye. While flattery will get you somewhere—though not everywhere with smart reporters— don't just use the mechanism to give bouquets. If you take issue with a story, say so. Or if you have some ideas on how to follow up on the story, tell them that too. It is the dialogue that is important. It indicates that you recognize their bylines and take an interest in what they do. You are interested in their brand, and want to help it become better and more competitive. You send the message that their art, their craft, is important to you.

## Summary of Trends

▶ *To manage the media, companies must understand the agendas of reporters and the outlets they represent.*

▶ *Most public relations people fail at media relations because they don't understand these agendas.* Companies must demand the same due diligence in this area as they do in their legal affairs.

▶ *Reporters' motivations are not what many company executives think they are.* They don't do what they do "to sell papers." Nor do they do what they do to make money—if they were motivated by money, they would probably pursue another more lucrative line of work.

▶ *Good newspapers and other media outlets separate the business and editorial sides of their operations.* It is important for readers and for attracting the best journalism talent.

▶ *Reporters seek information that will lead them to the truth, or as close to the truth as they can get using the resources on hand and on deadline.* For some, wrapping the truth in a well-told tale through good writing is a bonus.

▶ *In a competitive environment, reporters compete with rivals to get better information, closer to the truth, and a better story.* They do not care if their work ultimately helps their company sell more papers than that of their journalistic rival.

▶ *The byline is a reporter's brand.* It is the currency among journalists. It is their signature of their work and the recognition that their media outlets trust them enough to put their brand alongside their own.

## Lessons for Companies

▶ *Learn reporters' agendas.* Talk to them. Understand what motivates them. Make sure the other people in your company do, too. The same goes for your outside public relations agency or consultant, if you have one.

▶ *Don't suggest to reporters that their work sells papers.* That will indicate that you do not understand why they do the job they do and why they ask the questions they ask.

▶ *Don't assume that because you advertise with a media outlet you will get coverage of whatever you say.* And don't think that your advertising dollars will buy you favors in a time of crisis. Journalists, who have no interest in the business side of their employer, will treat you the same as they would any other company. They could resent your suggestion that they owe you a favor because you're an advertiser

▶ *Beware of getting caught in between competing reporters at the same outlet.* It may strain the relationship you have with a good contact. Their problem can quickly become your problem.

▶ *Don't underestimate a reporter's ability to get information quickly and completely.* Technology has compressed the time it takes a reporter to get a lot of information.

▶ *Open and maintain a personal dialogue with a reporter.* Personal, handwritten notes are best, especially in an era when technology has desensitized and impersonalized the world.

# Hitting the Iceberg

## Adding Media to Your Crisis Plan

I n early 1995, a *Business Week* reporter uncovered some interesting information about Bausch & Lomb, the big maker of eye care products. The reporter's sources told him that there were some irregularities in the accounting of the company's sales and revenues, particularly in the Asia Pacific region. Orders, he was told, were being booked as sales, giving an inflated picture of how well the company was doing. The suggestion, sources said, was that these irregularities were not simply the result of a few rogue salespeople trying to pump up sales to make themselves look good. Rather, the practice was systemic and institutionalized, the result of intense red-line pressure on salespeople to meet steep quotas. Those quotas, the sources said, originated at the highest levels of the company.

The reporter wrote a small article about the situation for *Business Week,* suggesting that the chairman, Daniel Gill, had a problem on his hands. Even if Gill had not sanctioned the practice, which would have been a serious charge, the chairman should have been aware that it was occurring.

So, the ball was in Bausch & Lomb's court. Here was a situation that could go either way. If the company acknowledged the problem and vowed to fix it immediately, the reporter would go away. Sure, the reporter might write a story that caused the company minor embarrassment, but the company would at least get good marks for acting quickly to right a wrong. Unfortunately for the company and for Gill, the situation went the other way. Rather, they took it the other way. Not only did the company deny the irregularities, it claimed the article was misleading. It wrote a scathing letter to the editor of Business Week, criticizing the story and the reporter.

In the meantime, more information was uncovered, including reports of sales calendars with red marks on them that showed the days when sales quotas had to be met by whatever means possible. More coverage followed, including more denials from the company. Soon enough, because of the scandal and Bausch & Lomb's nationally recognized brand name, other media picked up on it—namely, television. Network investigative reporters started sniffing around, asking questions, filing reports. So intense was the scrutiny and so steadfast was the company in denying any wrongdoing that Bausch & Lomb's public relations agency was ordered to keep all media out of the company's annual meeting in New York. One reporter, who had slipped past security unnoticed, was asked to leave before the presentation would begin.

In the end, the allegations were found to be true. Irregularities in accounting for orders and sales were discovered, and the practice proved to have been widely known throughout the company, including in its senior ranks. While Gill maintained he had not sanctioned the practice and indeed was unaware of it, the sentiment internally and externally was that as chairman, he should have known. Ignorance of wrongdoing was, in this case, not considered an adequate excuse.

Gill announced his retirement not long after the annual meeting. Whether his move had anything to do with the Business Week reports was never made clear. But what was clear was a situation that could have been resolved with only minor embarrassment escalated because the company's senior management failed to understand a basic rule in crisis communications: Perception is reality, regardless of the facts. It doesn't matter if you haven't done anything wrong if people think you have.

Remeber, no company can avoid hitting the iceberg of media crisis. The goal is to keep from sinking.

## Address the Perception, Not the Reality

The rule has been played out in every major corporate crisis in the last thirty years. Pick up any modern crisis public relations book and you will probably see case studies of the following big-name crises: the Tylenol tampering case; the Intel Pentium chip fiasco; the airline crashes of TWA, ValuJet, and Swiss Air; Ford's fiery Pintos; the food poisoning problems at Jack-in-the-Box; Union Carbide's Bhopal chemical plant disaster; Perrier's water scandal; Beech-Nut's apple juice scam; and the meltdown at the Three Mile Island nuclear power plant. They were all big problems for big companies. Some of them were the result of accidents; others were caused by the inability or unwillingness of the companies involved to come clean.

Tylenol and Swiss Air probably did the best jobs of managing crises because they understood that the public's perception of what was happening was more important than what was really happening. These companies understood that their responses had to be directed to these perceptions. The facts would take care of themselves and be reported anyway. Unlike Intel, Johnson & Johnson, the maker of Tylenol, didn't ignore its problem, which began with reports that bottles of the painkiller had been tampered with and that poison had been inserted somehow. People died. Despite the fact that the reports were limited to a few incidents, Johnson & Johnson immediately launched a recall of more than thirty million bottles of Tylenol, at a cost of $100 million. The perception was that because a few bottles had been tampered with, all bottles were suspect, and that was enough to prompt the company to take action. In consumers' minds, there was widespread tampering, whether that was a fact or not. Perception became reality, and Johnson & Johnson recognized it. In the end, the $100 million spent on the recall paid off. Tylenol sales rebounded to even higher levels than before.

Swiss Air, too, understood what was important to the families of the victims of its flight that crashed in the Atlantic Ocean
off Peggy's Cove, Nova Scotia, in 1998, killing all on board. With
the help of the big New York public relations agency, Hill &
Knowlton, the company immediately put into motion a campaign to attend to the shocked families on both sides of the
Atlantic. Senior officials of the airline flew to North America from
Switzerland to meet the American families of the victims, while
other executives stayed in Zurich to tend to those awaiting loved
ones who would never arrive. Each family was assigned a personal
liaison with the airline who was responsible for everything from
dispensing information to answering questions to helping make
travel, accommodations, and funeral arrangements. Each liaison
was given an open expense account to take care of the families—
everything from travel to meals to rental cars was handled and
paid for by the airline. The effect was amazing. Victims' families,
when interviewed by the media, actually praised Swiss Air and
thanked the airline for all that it had done. A friend of mine,
whose neighbor had lost a teen-age daughter on the flight, called
me one night after the families had returned home from the crash
site. "It's incredible," he said of a conversation he had had with
the parents. "I'd be mad as hell. But they kept saying how great
Swiss Air was, how well they had been treated. Someone's got
some damn good PR." He was right. Swiss Air, with the help of
Hill & Knowlton, understood that in such a tragic situation, nothing could bring back the loved ones, but something could be
done to show that those ultimately responsible for the accident
cared. It was a simple but effective effort. And it was based on
understanding human nature.

In contrast, the crash of TWA Flight 800 off Long Island was
an aviation disaster made worse by a public relations disaster. The
mishandling of the aftermath of the crash became as much an
issue and widely publicized media story as the crash itself. From
the first hours following the crash to the painful end of the investigation two years later, the management of the airline was criticized for being unresponsive and uncaring. There appeared to be

no crisis plan to implement as angry families and friends swarmed New York's JFK airport in the hours immediately after the crash seeking information. The company appeared dazed and confused. TWA did not appear able to respond to reality or perception. It was not malicious avoidance of the situation, but it was negligence, and the company's reputation suffered. The case is still held as an example of how not to handle a crisis.

## The Value of Good Crisis Communication

The most effective explanation and use of the perception-reality dichotomy of crisis communications comes from James Taylor, then the general manager of Hill & Knowlton in New York in the early 1990s. Taylor, like most good crisis counselors, is an expert at painting the big picture around the facts of a situation first. That is an important first step in a crisis because clients are usually so close to the situation and embroiled in politics or emotions that they have difficulty putting the problem in perspective.

On a cold late-winter day, Taylor and our team were summoned to the headquarters of a major health care insurance company to discuss what it considered to be a serious financial and reputational crisis. The company was attempting to implement a new payment system for doctors, one that would change the way physicians would be reimbursed by patients' health plans. Many of the doctors, however, were not pleased with the new system, saying it would be more cumbersome from an administrative standpoint, and some would actually lose money. In protest, many doctors pulled out of the insurer's network of preferred providers. Some had even gone to the press to talk about what a bad idea the new payment plan was and, in a more stinging criticism, said that it was actually jeopardizing the level of care for patients. The company was losing valuable members of its network as well as the patient revenues that came with them, and it was getting slammed in the newspapers for being unfair to doctors and putting its plan members—the patients—at risk.

The company was having difficulty understanding why this was such an issue and why the doctors were making such a fuss. If the doctors looked at the situation as the company had presented it, the new plan was actually better. From an administrative point of view, it would be easier to manage, not more difficult. The doctors would have a more efficient way of getting paid; they would get paid faster and on a more regular basis. The notion that they would lose money did not compute with company officials. And, they said, if the doctors, plan members, and media looked at it properly, the level of care would actually improve because of the improved efficiencies of the system.

For several hours, at a crowded boardroom table in the company's suburban New York offices, company officials eagerly laid out the issues for us and explained that the doctors simply didn't get it. They kept beating their heads wondering why the doctors couldn't see it their way. The situation was emotionally charged because more doctors were leaving the network every day, and a group of doctors serving a very affluent section of the metropolitan area was threatening to walk as well.

Taylor listened, then spoke. The problem was one of perception versus reality. And somewhere in between lay the answer to the crisis. To startle them out of their boxed-in thinking, he took a black magic marker and drew a big circle and a big square on a pad at the end of the room. "In the fourteenth century," he began, "when Genoese sailors set out to find the new world, they thought the world looked like this," and he pointed to the square. "It wasn't until they had sailed around the world and made it home without falling off that they realized it looked like this," he said, pointing to the circle. The clients were fascinated. To break the tension, one even asked him if our recommendation was to use some fourteenth-century Genoese sailors to solve the crisis. The jab was a welcome comic break in the intensity.

The point, Taylor continued, was that the company knew the world was round, but the doctors thought the world was flat. The company thought the new payment plan was better. The doctors thought it was worse. To them, the perception was the reality. The breakdown was in the communications effort the company had used to inform the doctors about the benefits of the new plans. A review of the effort turned up the problem. The company really had done very little to explain the new plan to the doctors. The most significant form of correspondence was a terse letter from the chief executive outlining the new structure and saying that it would be implemented on a certain date. Very little effort had been made to help the doctors understand why the new system was better for all concerned. From the doctors' point of view, the company was simply shoving something new down their throats. Some doctors felt that the fact that the company didn't take the time to explain why the plan was better, indicated that it was worse. Remember, if people don't have the facts, they will fill in the hole in a story with speculation, usually negative. Uncertainty drives fear, which prompts people to expect the worst.

In the end, the standoff was like an old fashioned strike—company against union members. And this company had acted as if it were an old-style industrial concern, issuing an edict that things would change without offering any explanations. The big problem: These doctors were no dummies, and they had other choices. They were not bound to this company at all. There were plenty of other insurers out there who would treat them better and allow them to make a decent living as well.

So the plan, really, was simple. Convince the doctors that the new plan was better. Educate them. Inform them. Show them in detail how the whole thing worked. Work with them as partners instead of imposing things on them from on high. Treat them with respect, not only because they are doctors, but also because they are virtual employees of the company. The problem, of course, was that there was so much ill will between the two sides that they had to work twice as hard to convince the doctors, their patients, and the media about the worth of the plan. From a communications standpoint, the effort was something the company should have undertaken at the very start. Its arrogance and misreading of its own power and influence created a problem—a crisis—that did not need to occur. And now, it was faced with convincing a bunch of angry, untrusting Genoese sailors that the world was round.

## Business Problem or Communication Problem?

There's another important crisis message in this example, and one of the first things a company should think about when confronted with a crisis. It will have a huge impact on how effective your crisis communications plan is. In fact, it should be the starting point of any crisis program. When things go wrong, first ask yourself: Is this a business problem or a communications problem? What's the difference? A lot. A business problem cannot be fixed with good communications. It cannot be resolved with spin. If a company does something wrong or something goes wrong at a company, you cannot cover it up or make it look like something it's not. The media are too smart. They have too many tools at their disposal with which to find the truth. They have become pretty good at sniffing out phonies. I remember while I was at *The Miami Herald,* one of my regular contacts was the spokesperson for a large airline. He was a well-meaning fellow whose idea of public relations was to live in denial. The joke about him was that even if he was filmed by a television camera while standing in front of the burning wreckage of one of his company's airliners, his comment would be: "What crash?" And consumers of media are too smart, as well, to fall for fakery.

Yet, you will see people in companies across the country who, when faced with business problems, ask public relations people to solve them. Lawyers are often the ones who get themselves in the worst trouble. Maybe because they talk almost as much as PR people, if not more. The difference is, however, that the lawyer's argument may be heard by only a few people. The public relations person's argument may be heard by millions.

Here's an example: The general counsel of a client company came to me once for help. An employee, it seemed, had done some bad things. He had gone to a bar in his bright red sports car, gotten drunk, and tried to buy drugs from a woman at the bar. It turned out the woman was an undercover police officer working a drug sweep, and he was nabbed. Complicating the situation was the fact that the employee held a fairly prominent position in the company—not at the senior management level—but he generated enough sales that he was considered a keeper. It would be a shame if his misdeeds were reported in the newspapers and tarnished his firm's name. But reporters had already been calling. The general counsel had their names written on a piece of paper he clutched in his hand. Would I call them, he asked, and tell them it's not a story? And if they didn't believe me, would I call their editors and tell them that their reporters would be irresponsible if they wrote the story, and the paper equally irresponsible if it published the story? Could I call anyone, anywhere who could be manipulated?

Well, of course, the answer was no. I would call the reporter to get a sense of what the gist of the story would be and try to gauge the prominence it might get, but unless I were in a position to deny all the facts in the police report about our employee, it would be very difficult to make it go away. It was an occupational hazard. People do dumb things. Accidents happen. That's what makes news. No amount of spin is going to change that.

## Spin Doctoring

Spin, according to the New York public relations guru, Robert Dilenschneider, "is bad for you; it's bad for your company, and (if you're a public relations professional) it's bad for your clients." In a 1998 presentation called "Spin: A High-Risk Strategy" to the Bulldog Reporter and PR Newswire Media Relations Conference, Dilenschneider said that "spin corrupts. It is wrong, and ultimately counter-productive." He defined spin as "a deliberate and reckless disregard for the truth. I find spin offensive and destructive to (the public relations) profession. Spin doctoring is to public relations what pornography is to art. Spin doctoring is to public relations what quackery is to medicine." He goes on to quote the results of a series of interviews he conducted during his research. The results are fascinating:

> ▶ *A newspaper reporter from a major national newspaper:* "The dictionary says spin can stand for fabrication by process of the mind or imagination. That's right on target. Spin doctors work with myth, not with facts."

> ▶ *A hedge fund manager:* "I manage over 500 million dollars. But I have to be careful in every regard. I resent any effort to spin me and believe that it is illegal and unethical as well."

> ▶ *The editor of a major business magazine:* "We know spin when we see it. And we're seeing more of it today than ever before. I think there are some public relations people and their companies and clients who have become so desperate to gain exposure, they'll take shortcuts to the truth. To them, the end justifies the means. Spin is self-defeating in the long run. It wins some battles but loses the war."

In crisis situations the same is true. You cannot appear on camera in front of a burning aircraft and deny that anything has happened. Nor can you embellish facts to make yourself look better or make a bad situation look not so bad. You just read the comments from smart people. They get it. They see through it. If you saw the movie "Wag the Dog," you know what spin is all about and why, despite its apparent success in the movie, it is a risky proposition. To make your spin plan work, you don't want to have to kill Dustin Hoffman at the end of the day.

There persists in Corporate America a belief that as a public relations person it is who you know at a newspaper that can help you avoid damaging crisis situations. This is simply not true. But it is because of this belief that a lot of companies hire former journalists as public relations people. Senior executives believe that in times of trouble, the journalist-turned-PR person can simply pick up the phone and call his or her friends at the paper to kill the story. My client's general counsel believed the same thing when he asked me to make the embarrassing story about the salesman go away. And it's a bit of a cruel joke, because many wide-eyed, well-intentioned journalists who take the bait and go into public relations think that they are being hired for skills in writing and thinking and don't realize they are being hired for their contacts. If you are a company executive, don't fall into this trap for two reasons. First, contacts change, especially in the modern media environment. Reporters come and go, beats change. If you invest in a journalist as a public relations person, you had better make sure he or she has more than an address book because it will become obsolete pretty fast. Second, and more important, no reporter, friend or foe, unless ethically unsound, is going to kill a story that has real news value and substantiating facts. Reporters may sit on a story—delay its release—if you can prove to them that you have facts that could render it untrue. But don't count it, and don't play that game too often. Remember, in the world of relationships with the media, credibility is your only form of currency. And once it's lost, it's difficult, if not impossible, to get it back. You may pull a fast one on a reporter once, but be aware of the adage, once burned, twice shy. As Dilenschneider pointed out, spin wins some battles but loses the war.

In the end, a public relations person's contacts are only as good as his or her own credibility and ability to understand the agendas of the reporters with whom he or she is dealing. There is no easy way out of a bad situation. The best thing you can do is be prepared in advance, understand the nature of the problem, and work to minimize the damage. Don't risk blowing your credibility or that of your company by playing a losing game of spin the issue. It will not pay off.

In determining whether a crisis is a business problem or a communications problem, understanding the type of problem you face will help you determine the type of solution you should implement. In the health-care company example, they had a communications problem that led to a business problem. The Bausch & Lomb example was a business problem that became a communications problem because of the company's efforts at spin—it attempted to obfuscate the truth.

## Know When to Shut Up

When you have determined the nature of the problem, the trick is to determine the appropriate response, if any. In an environment of plenty, there is often a temptation to say too much. And in an environment where spin has become dangerous and a liability, sometimes it pays to say nothing at all. I had a client who loved the media and would talk with them any chance he got. In this case, the challenge was to stifle his tendancy to talk and keep him out of trouble. Here's what happened: His company was preparing for an initial public offering that promised to be big news. The buzz surrounding the IPO was deafening, and he was ecstatic. On the eve of the offering, however, something went very wrong. My client's largest competitor, which was considerably larger, announced that it was drastically reducing the prices on its competing line of consumer products. The market and the media went crazy. This was big competitive news. My client, naturally, had to match the price cut on his product line to remain competitive. On the day of the IPO, the big news was the price wars between the competitors, with my client's rival getting top billing. The IPO, despite its success, played second fiddle.

There were many good reasons for my client to keep quiet and control his obvious anger. The first was that the competitor's trick was a perfectly predictable tactic in a very competitive business. It wasn't illegal, and it wasn't unfair. In fact, it was pretty smart, competitively. But if my client went to the media and complained about how mean it was, he would probably be the laughingstock of the industry. I shuddered thinking about the headlines: "Crybaby CEO Cries Foul," or "One-Upped CEO Asks, What About Me?" But there was another and even more compelling reason to zip his lip. Under the rules of the Securities and

Exchange Commission, no one at a company that has just made a public offering may speak publicly about its merits until thirty days after the date of the IPO. The logic is that a new offering must find its own place to settle in the market, without excess hype, without manipulation. The client eventually took my advice and let off steam on the tennis court. But I would rather have been pelted by 130-mile-an-hour forehand smashes than try to rebuild the company's credibility if the crybaby story had appeared—or worse, to have appeared before the SEC to explain why we had violated the quiet-period rules of public discussion. The world, I guess, is full of trade-offs.

The point is, know when to hold and when to fold. Keep a cool head in a crisis, and don't shoot your mouth off and get yourself into more trouble. Equally important, don't be bullied by the media. Just because they are pounding on your door and screaming about being on deadline, take your time. Make sure any response is reasoned and credible. Remember, it is much harder to correct a mistake than to get it right the first time.

## Being Prepared by Having a Plan

Crisis relations people will tell you that all you need is a plan. And you can have one designed and ready to go fairly inexpensively. It is typically logistical—it includes key contact numbers, central meeting places where decision makers can gather, and lists of key media contacts to be contacted first with important information. If yours is a large company, you probably already have a contingency plan for a business crisis. If yours is a small company, you probably don't. A crisis plan doesn't need to be elaborate. It is really all about being prepared. In a crisis, the biggest liability is silence because no matter what the problem, the media needs to fill space and time. If your company isn't there to provide information, the emptiness will be filled with conjecture.

Being prepared for a crisis really begins long before the problem arises and involves far more than a binder full of phone and fax numbers. At the core of an effective plan is a person, or small group of people, who will become the crisis team. Among the team members should be the senior executives, particularly the chief executive, a communications person, and any specialist or professional who can provide technical information and guidance if necessary. As the leader of the team, choose a person who will act as the point through which all information will flow—both in and out. This is important not only to make sure your messages are consistent but also to gauge the public's and media's reaction to the crisis. Make sure you and all the senior managers know how to reach this person at all times—and he or she knows how to reach you. And make sure this person develops relationships with key contacts who cover your company. If you get vital information to your most influential media outlets first, the random media outlets that may be drawn to the story will follow their lead and seek out their opinions for context. In such cases, make your best media work for you. Tee them up as a resource for the other media that pile on if the crisis spreads beyond your company's normal universe. To make sure this is effective, update your media lists. Make sure you know who your key contacts are and how to reach them in a hurry. And make sure they know how to reach your key contacts, too. Crises rarely occur between 9 and 5.

Another important preparatory step of your plan should be the selection of a central place, off the site of your company if necessary, where the key crisis team can gather if things go wrong. In fact, it's not a bad idea to have a couple of contingencies. If a crisis occurs offsite, designate in advance a place in your office building to set up a command center. Make sure it has the necessary infrastructure and communications equipment—telephones, fax machines, televisions, radio, and computers. If your company does not have another site to go to, consider a hotel. Contact the managers of a couple of hotels near your office and tell them that in the event of a crisis, you would like to use their facilities if they have availability. Most hotels will be happy to accommodate you if they can. If you live in a large city like New York or Los Angeles, there are companies from which you can lease suites of offices for just these purposes. Many are retained on a contract basis and are not particularly expensive—they operate a little like a timeshare. This small investment could save your company in the event of a crisis. And if you never have to use it, consider it a worthwhile insurance policy.

At the same time, if you have operations in other cities, have updated transportation schedules to all of these cities as part of your crisis plan. If a plant exploded a thousand miles away in the middle of the night, you would need to know how to get your crisis people there in a hurry. And make sure these facilities have crisis plans, including off-site places to go, as well.

Throughout the planning process, don't forget your internal audience—your employees. Make sure that you set up a special communications system to keep them informed. This is important for several reasons. First, you owe it to them. They are, in effect, family members of the company. They have a vested interest in the company. Some of them are shareholders. Second, they must be assured that a crisis situation is under control or your entire operation could shut down. A crisis will distract employees—even those not in the affected facilities. They will divert their attention from the tasks at hand to find out what's going on. If you can keep them up to date about a situation, they will remain calm and focused. And third, view every employee as a potential spokesperson. In many cases, the media will seek out employees for reaction stories. In crisis situations, the reality is that you can throw the media policy book out the window. Excitement, fear, adrenaline will all prompt people—even the most closed-mouth ones—to talk. When the television light goes on and the microphone is pushed to their lips, fifteen minutes—or more precisely—fifteen seconds of fame await. It's human nature for them to respond. There's not much you can do about it.

Don't forget media training as part of the crisis preparation plan. This is vital. Good trainers will specialize in crisis media training. Don't think that if you've had regular media training that you're prepared. You need to get the experience, or at least simulated experience, in what's it's like in the heat of battle. Remember, there are certain crisis situations that you simply cannot man-

age from your office chair. You will have to have a press conference. You may be on location at a plant or other facility where
you are the center of a media scrum—a large group of reporters
firing off questions one after the other or, more likely, all at once.
You may also be faced with demonstrators or angry customers
who will complicate the mix. You must learn how to think on
your feet, deliver your messages, and maintain your composure.
You must exude confidence and assure your important audiences
that things are under control.

## Keeping the Message Brief and Accurate

If a crisis hits, and you are prepared, the process logistics should
take care of themselves. When you have determined the nature of
the crisis—business or communication—and have decided that
you are going to respond through whatever method the situation
demands—press conference, press release, teleconference or
another method—you need to decide on some key messages.
They should be brief and easily digestible, especially for the
broadcast media. They should be clear and free of jargon, and
there should be only three or four of them—any more and the
media will lose track. They should be geared toward assuring the
public that the company is aware of the problem and moving
quickly to fix it. As well, it should give as much information as
possible without jeopardizing any investigations or legal actions
that may arise later. Be careful on this point. In the early stages of
a crisis, especially a disaster, information is often unreliable. It may
be coming from a highly confused, emotionally charged environment. Do not release any information that has not been confirmed. And don't deal in speculation. You may feel you are being
helpful to the media by guessing about what happened or what
might happen next. It will hurt you in the end.

   If the crisis is rather slow moving—such as a lawsuit—and
will unfold over time, you may have time to prepare a Q&A document that will help your spokespeople anticipate the media
response. The answers may also help in the development of your

key messages. A useful tool in a crisis is a worst-case scenario article. In an earlier chapter, we looked at how such an article prepared for a client stopped him from making a crisis situation even worse. In a crisis, such a document can test your messages and help you see how they might appear in the media. If you consider that a press release is a best-case scenario—it is exactly how you would like your story to appear—a worst case shows you how your messages will probably be put into context by the media, once they have talked to others involved in the situation and searched the data bases for information that may suggest your crisis is not an isolated incident but a pattern of negligence.

Throughout a crisis situation, remember to be flexible. A crisis plan must be able to adapt to new angles, related problems, and so-called aftershocks. A crisis plan that is too rigid can make matters worse because it stops your response mechanism dead.

If you are part of a small company, you may be saying that all of this elaborate planning is not necessary. But size is no guarantee of anonymity. If you are a public company, you must take steps to protect your investment and those of your shareholders in the event of the unexpected. And, presumably, you will not always be a small company. You probably have a growth plan, which should include a communications plan to build a brand identity. An important part of building and protecting that brand is crisis communications, which is why the big companies with the household names have—or should have—crisis plans. If they are effective, and if you are true to yourself and your audiences about what is going on, you can survive a crisis with your brand and reputation intact. A question posed in an October 1995 article in the American Management Association's *Management Review* should be considered by every chief executive officer of every company, large, medium, or small: "The landscape is littered with organizations that were injured or killed by bad press in emergency situations. But there are also numerous examples of those that survived and bounced back following a mishap. In the face of a disaster, which kind of organization would you be?"

## Summary of Trends

▶ *The biggest mistake companies make in crisis situations is addressing the reality, rather than the perception of a situation.* The facts mean nothing if the public doesn't believe them.

▶ *Companies have still not learned that it is impossible to hide the truth in a crisis situation.* In doing so, they only make the situation worse.

▶ *Technology has allowed bad news to travel farther faster.* As a result, crisis containment is more difficult than ever.

▶ *Reporters are taking advantage of technology to conduct more in-depth investigation.* They have more information at their fingertips, making hiding information more difficult.

## Lessons for Companies

▶ *Determine if the crisis is a business problem or a communications problem.* A business problem cannot be solved by communications, no matter how good your relationships with the media.

▶ *Avoid trying to spin bad news.* It doesn't work, and in the end, it may actually make a bad situation worse. The media and your other audiences are too smart to fall for fakery.

▶ *Relationships with the media are only as good as the credibility of your public relations people.* It's not who you know, it's whether reporters will believe you when you tell them something.

▶ *Prepare a crisis plan.* It does not have to be elaborate. Be organized, select a crisis team, choose fully wired command centers on site and off site. Update your media lists. If you have field operations, make sure you know how to get to them quickly, and make sure they have crisis plans and facilities lined up too.

▶ *Put your senior people through crisis media training.* Make this a mandatory part of your plan.

▶ *Develop key messages.* Make sure they focus on control and solutions to the problem. Don't be afraid to not say much or to say nothing at all if the situation warrants.

▶ *In a crisis, don't be bullied by the media.* Give reasoned responses. Don't distribute unconfirmed or incomplete information. Don't guess or speculate about what happened or what might happen.

▶ *In a slow-moving crisis, use question-and-answer documents and worst-case scenario mock-up articles to test your messages.*

# CONCLUSION

I f anything you have just read is unfamiliar to you, or frightens you a little, don't feel bad. You are not alone. The rise of the business news media, the emergence of the consumer-investor, and the technological miracles that have opened up the world into a twenty-four-hours-a-day, seven-days-a-week super-store of information and opinion have occurred almost overnight. So swift are the changes that even companies considered to be leaders in communications are scrambling to keep up. Consumers of news, too, are overwhelmed with information overload, uncertain about what's reliable and what's not. And yes, even the media are having difficulty keeping up with their own growth in terms of finding talent to keep the big new media pipeline full of credible and useful information. Everyone on all sides of the new media equation is struggling to keep pace.

If you manage a company, whether small, medium, or large, there are a couple of things you need to do to make sure the gap between what you know and what you don't know doesn't get wider. Because if it does, the consequences can be serious. And in an environment where the media are a major determining factor in the success or failure of your company's brand image, you can't afford to ignore what's going on.

First, make sure you incorporate communications, particularly media relations, into your strategic business plan. Communications should be as important as manufacturing, sales, and distribution. Through communications, including many of the aspects touched upon in this book, you can stay plugged in. Remember, when done properly, communications can be an excellent way to get your messages out and to receive information and insight from the environment in which you do business. A communications effort does not need to be elaborate. But you must get started. You must be a part of this new environment. Every day you lose, you fall farther behind.

Second, get professional communications help if you don't already have it. Consider good communications and relationships with the media to be as serious an issue as any other in your business. You wouldn't think of attempting a merger or acquisition without an investment bank. You wouldn't think of making a substantial investment for your company without the support of a financial advisor. You wouldn't tackle a serious legal issue without legal counsel. The same goes for the media. Theirs is a specialized world that requires specialists to manage on your behalf. A reliable public relations agency or consultant can put together an effective plan, including proactive, reactive, and crisis elements, at a relatively modest cost—far less than the cost of an advertising campaign.

The benefits of understanding and engaging in the new media environment are many. It is an exciting, dynamic place that opens up a world of opportunity for companies to gain exposure and build brand recognition. But it is also a world filled with pitfalls that can derail and damage even the best-laid plans. The point is that companies no longer have the choice of whether to engage the media or not. Whether companies like it or not, the media are paying attention to them. And that in itself should be enough of a wake-up call to prompt companies, including yours, to act.

# INDEX

accuracy, 214–215
advertising, 5, 55
Amazon.com, 163–165
America Online (AOL), 90–91
audience(s), media, 125–143
  and audits, 137–141
  and choice, 133–136
  educating, 44–47
  expectations of, 30–31
  gauging opinions of,
    126–128
  internal, 128–131
  strategy for communicating
    with, 131–133
  surveying, 136–141
audits, 137–141
avoiding the media, 150–152

baby boom generation, 4
Barron's, 3, 6, 163–164
Bartiromo, Maria, 24
Bausch & Lomb, 199–200
Bezos, Jeff, 163–164
Blockbuster Entertainment
  Corp., 133–134
Bloomberg, Michael, 26–27
brands, building, 128
brevity, 214–215
Brigham, Tom, on CEOs' view
  of PR, 187
Brokaw, Tom, on information
  cycle, 54
business development scams,
  91–95
Business Week, 3, 6, 37,
  41–43, 120, 199, 200
Business Week Online, 28
bylines, 190–194

Case, Steve, 90–91
Cavuto, Neil, 24
"CBS Evening News," 105
CBSMarketWatch, 28
"CEO stars," 30
changes in business news
  media, 1–2
Charles Schwab, 109
"The Charlie Rose Show,"
  27–28, 175–176
Chase Manhattan, 35
chat rooms, Internet, 8
China, 5
Clinton, Bill, 25, 41, 91, 120,
  129–130, 153
CNBC, 3, 24, 27, 106, 120,
  173
CNN, 2, 3, 120
"CNN Moneyline," 24, 105,
  112
communication(s), 219–220
  crisis, 203–207
  and employees, 12
  and growth strategy, 11
  with media audiences,
    131–133
company spokespersons, see
  spokespersons
competitive pressures, 36–37,
  41, 193
consumer-investors, 3, 6, 13,
  29, 107–109, 116–117
contacts, media, 153–155
Cramer, James, 27, 28
credibility, media, 53–65,
  152–153
  and advertising, 55
  examples of, 53–54, 58–61

*credibility, media (cont.)*
  and information cycle,
    54–55
  popular beliefs about,
    56–57
  and use of media, 61–63
crisis relations, 199–217
  brevity/accuracy in,
    214–215
  and communications plan,
    203–207
  and perception, 201–203
  plans for, 211–214
  silence in, 210–211
  and spin doctoring,
    207–210
Crooke, Robert A., 54

demographic trends, 4
Dilenschneider, Robert, on
  spin, 207–209
distrust of media, 56–57
Dobbs, Lou, 24, 105, 106,
  122
Doherty, Jacqueline, 163, 164
Dresdner Bank, 67–68
Dunlap, Al, 148–149

E. F. Hutton, 110
Edgar, 69
employees, and communica-
  tions, 12
entertainment
  business news as, 17–34
  development of, 20–23
  in mainstream media,
    27–28
  and personalities, 26–27
  and role of spokespeople,
    28–33
  and "Wall Street," 23–26
"Entertainment Tonight," 18

errors, journalistic, 10
executives, senior,
  as spokespersons, 166–168
  women, 21–22

Farrell, Mary, 172–174
financial services industry, as
  mass consumer business, 6
*Financial Times,* 120
*Financial World,* 6
*Forbes,* 6
*Fortune,* 6, 11–12, 25
401(k) plans, 4
Fox, 2
Fox News, 3, 24

Gallup Organization, 4, 40,
  108, 120
Geddes, John, 113–114
Gekko, Gordon, 23–24
Generation X, 69
Gharib, Suzie, 24
Gill, Daniel, 199–200
Greenspan, Alan, 106
Grove, Andrew, 8, 90
growth strategies, 10–11

Hershey, Robert D., on
  Internet stock trading, 5
Hill & Knowlton, 202, 203
Huizenga, Wayne, 133–135

ignorance
  in business news reporting,
    35–51
  and competitive pressures,
    36–37, 41
  education as defense
    against, 44–47
  and lack of reporting talent,
    39–41, 47–49
  and rumors, 37–38

Individual Retirement
  Accounts (IRAs), 4
information cycle, 54–55
Intel Corporation, 8, 88–90
internal audiences, 128–131
Internet, 2
  chat rooms on, 8
  stock trading over, 5,
  109–111
investing, 4
Investor's Business Daily, 115–116
IRAs (Individual Retirement
  Accounts), 4

Japan, 5
Johnson & Johnson, 201
Jordan, Michael, 174–175
journalists
  bylines of, 190–194
  errors by, 10
  Internet access by, 71
  use of online tools by, 70
  use of Web by, 73
  see also reporters

Kennedy, John F., Jr., 61
Kiplinger's, 3
Kmart, 18–19
Kungas, Paul, 24

Lawrence, David, 145
Lewinsky, Monica, 25, 91, 153

Manning, Bert, on media
  credibility, 55
Maples, Marla, 146
Marron, Donald B., 120, 121
  on changes in modern
  investing environment, 107
  on resignation of Robert
  Rubin, 105–106
  on 1990s, 4

Media in Cyberspace Study,
  67, 69–77
"me" media, 87–88, 91–92
Merrill Lynch, 35, 109
The Miami Herald, 145–147, 206
Middleberg, Don, 71, 73–75
Middleberg + Associates, 79
monitoring services, online,
  99–101
mutual funds, 4, 5

NASDAQ, 115
National Transportation Safety
  Board (NTSB), 61
Newsday, 63
newspapers, 6–7, 70–71
  see also specific papers
The New York Daily News, 63,
  181–183
The New York Post, 63,
  181–183
The New York Times, 3, 10, 22,
  25, 45–47, 54, 58, 63, 77,
  78, 112–116, 120,
  156–157, 186–187
"Nightly Business Report,"
  112
Norris, Floyd, 115, 116
NTSB (National Transportation
  Safety Board), 61

O'Donnell, Rosie, 17–18
O'Neill, William, 115–116
online news reporting, 67–85
  and business development
  scams, 91–95
  and company policies, 97–99
  by inexperienced reporters,
  77–78
  and Internet pranksters,
  95–97
  managing, 78–80

online news reporting (cont.)
  Media in Cyberspace Study
    on, 69–77
  monitoring of, 99–101
  by nonjournalists, 87–103
  as phenomenon, 68–69
  speed of, 67–68
online news services, 2, 8–10
online policies, 97–99
online trading, growth of, 5,
    109–111
opinion journalism, 9
opportunities, media,
    156–157
overexposure, 7

PaineWebber, 37–38, 40–43,
    67–68, 96, 98, 107–109,
    117–122, 191–192
PaineWebberGroup Inc., 4
PBS, 120, 173
"PBS Nightly Business
    Report," 24
Pentium chip, 8, 88–90
perception, reality vs.,
    201–203
policies, online, 97–99
pranksters, online, 95–97
Purcell, Philip J., 19, 25

reporters
  and editorial vs. business
    functions, 188–190
  inexperienced, 77–78
  motivations of, 185–188
  talent deficit among, 39–41,
    47–49
  and technology, 194–195
  understanding, 184–185
  see also journalists
Reuters, 32
Rice, Jerry, 175

Rivera, Geraldo, 19
Rivers, Joan, 176–177
Rose, Charlie, 27–28,
    175–176
Ross, Steven S., 10, 67, 70–71
Rubin, Robert, 105–106, 122
Rukeyser, Louis, 25
rumors, 38–39

Salinger, Pierre, 58
scams, business development,
    91–95
Securities and Exchange
    Commission (SEC), 69,
    210–211
Selleck, Tom, 17–18
senior executives, as
    spokespersons, 166–168
Sheen, Charlie, 23
silence, value of, 210–211
"Siskel and Ebertizing of
    America," 5–6, 55
Smart Money, 3, 112
Social Security, 4, 108
Sommers, Larry, 105
spin doctoring, 207–210
spokespersons, 163–179
  and business news as enter-
    tainment, 28–33
  choosing, 157–159,
    165–166
  senior executives as,
    166–168
  skill of, 170–172, 174–178
  subject areas for, 31–32
  training of, 168–170,
    172–174
Stern, Howard, 18
stock trading, Internet, 5,
    109–111
Sunbeam, 148–149
surveys, 136–141

Swiss Air, 201, 202

targeting, media, 7–8
Taylor, James, 203–205
 on building a brand, 128
 on "Siskel and Ebertizing of
  America," 5–6
technology, 7, 69, 80, 81,
 184, 194–195
TheStreet.com, 3, 28
TJRF Group, 184
training, media, 168–170,
 172–174, 213–214
Trump, Donald, 145–148
Trump, Ivana, 146
TWA Flight 800, 58–61,
 202–203
"two friends" theory, 12
Tylenol tampering case, 201

USA Today, 120
use of media
 and credibility, 61–63
 effective, 3–4

vacuum, media as, 12–13

"Wag the Dog," 208

Wall Street, 105–123
 consolidation on, 109
 and consumer-investors,
  107–109, 116–117
 and growth of online
  trading, 109–111
 in-house PR management
  on, 118–122
 New York Times coverage of,
  113–116
 transformation of, into
  media object, 106–107,
  112–113
"Wall Street" (film), 23–26
The Wall Street Journal, 3, 6,
 10, 25, 35, 36, 38, 40, 46,
 63, 81, 112–117, 192
The Wall Street Journal
 Interactive Edition, 28
"Wall Street Week," 112, 173
Walsh, John J., on purpose of
 news, 19–20
The Washington Post, 57, 120,
 150–151
Web sites, 71, 95
women executives, 21–22

Y2K, 92–94